Steve—Thanks for being such a great friend! I aspire to be 1% of the writer you are.

YOU SOUND Amazing!

Every Single Lie of the Music Business

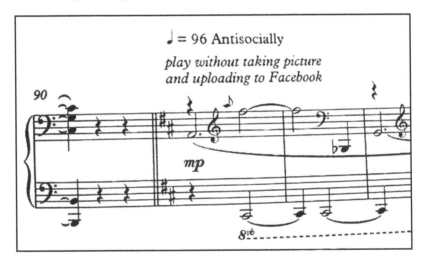

♩ = 96 Antisocially

play without taking picture and uploading to Facebook

90

mp

8vb

(AND a whole lot more!)

Jeffrey WeBer

20/100

illustrated By BoB Wynne

Headline Books, Inc.
Terra Alta, WV

You Sound Amazing! Every Single Lie of the Music Business
(And a whole lot more!)

by Jeffrey Weber

illustrated by Bob Wynne

To order additional copies of this book or for book publishing information, or to contact the author:

Headline Books, Inc.
P.O. Box 52
Terra Alta, WV 26764
www.HeadlineBooks.com

Tel: 304-789-3001
Email: mybook@headlinebooks.com

ISBN 13: 9781951556228

Library of Congress Control Number: 2020943837

Weber, Jeffrey
You Sound Amazing! Every Single Lie Of The Music Business
    p. cm.
    ISBN: 9781951556228
Humor 2. Music 3. Music Business 4. Weber, Jeffrey
Non-Fiction
Printed in The United States of America
First Edition
10 9 8 7 6 5 4 3 2 1

For my universal truths –
Michelle, Jerold, Jason, Jayme,
Jordan, Madison and Cole

Foreword

My favorite musician's joke concerns the little boy who says to his mother, "When I grow up, I want to be a musician"—to which she replies, with an indulgent smile, "Now dear, you know you can't do both."

Jeff Weber has done the next best thing: he almost grew up, and he became a music producer. (Of real and famous musicians, too! You could look it up.) And he has lived to tell about it.

In the process, he has collected enough good stories, stumbled upon enough priceless documents, cataloged enough memorable lists and one-liners, and encountered enough casual mendacity to write two books—which in fact he did, in 2012 and 2015. Then he decided that even two books couldn't quite contain the full range of seedy misinformation, perfidious treachery, and heartbreaking small-mindedness on this subject. Hence this final catch all and tell all.

He could have called it *You've Got A Deal 3! More Biggest Lies,* etc. etc. But he didn't want people to confuse it with the movie business, which is the one industry that can lay claim to even more and bigger lies than the music biz—and even less imagination when it comes to finding titles for sequels. So, he didn't do that.

I know a lot of people in the arts—actors, painters, writers, a sculptor or two, and even a couple of performance artists (heaven forfend)—and they all find their own ways of dealing with the looming poverty that follows most artists like a needy ex. But none of them come close to the bitingly honest, blisteringly sardonic humor that musicians have developed. It could be that few artists besides musicians have to combat such a long line of sleazy managers, grubby agents, penny-pinching presenters, and record-business execs who long ago forgot how to distinguish convenient lies from fundamental truths. Or that no other artists base their profession on playing one night here followed by one night there—usually at least a day's drive from "here"—only to end up with a few hours' sleep in a crummy fleabag, in order to take the stage to play brilliantly in front of people drinking the night away. Or that few other professions with such an ancient and noble tradition attract such an array of variably talented wannabes.

Whatever the reason, musicians' humor has its own history and customs, its special mores and ethos, and plenty of pain peeking through the laughter. Or should that be the other way around?

Sometimes it's hard to tell. But one thing I know for sure: the laughter is there. It might elicit a guffaw, or a groan, or a wry smile, or a stabbing insight, all of which you'll find within these pages. You may even glimpse the reason that so many have practiced so long to play so many notes for so little reward. (Actually, you can't miss it, since it's right there in the *Introduction*.)

Place this book somewhere handy, and make a point of consulting it, a few pages at a time, on a regular basis. If you're a musician, you'll appreciate its true-to-life wisdom. If you're *not* a musician, you'll at least understand why your musician friends talk the way they talk and think the way they think. And if you decide you really don't like being the adult in the room, you can always take up an instrument.

NEIL TESSER
June 2019

Neil Tesser has written on and broadcast jazz in Chicago for more than forty years, in media ranging from the *Chicago READER* to *USA Today* to National Public Radio to the *New York Times* to *Playboy Magazine*. He is the author of *The Playboy Guide to Jazz* (1998) and has authored liner notes for approximately 400 albums, receiving both a Grammy® award and the ASCAP Deems Taylor Award for this work. Also, his fantasy baseball team has finished first in two of the last three years. (And of course, that's where the REAL money is.)

"The world is a hellish place, and bad writing is destroying the quality of our suffering."

—Tom Waits

"Never, in all our history of popular music, has there been such a plethora of composers—professional, amateur, alleged— as we have today. Responsible, of course, are those two fresh hotbeds, the coniferous cinema and the radio.

The merciless ether - by unceasing plugging - has cut down the life of a popular song to but a few weeks, with the result that anyone who thinks he can carry a tune—even if it's nowhere in particular—nowadays takes a 'shot' at music-making."

—George Gershwin, May 1930
(Ranting about the glut of music in the
New York World Sunday Magazine)

"The music business is a cruel and shallow money trench, a long plastic hallway where thieves and pimps run free, and good men die like dogs. There's also a negative side."

—Hunter S. Thompson

contents

Introduction

WT⬛?

I read such a wonderfully poignant description of musicians and singers by David Ackert that I have re-printed it below, but it got me thinking…

We are in the midst of a significant transition from ownership to access. For many of us, we would prefer to own our music. Pay for it once and it's ours forever. But, for an increasing number of people, as long as they have access to their music, there is a belief that absolute ownership isn't necessary. Paying a small monthly fee, or a subscription, as it is now referred to, has become, to a growing audience, the accepted means of consumption.

Regardless of the way people discover and enjoy music, as producers, we pride ourselves in the great care we take in recording and manufacturing our music and will continue to do so. Period. We demand that the sonics be stunning, the lyrics be emotionally engaging and that the musicianship be jaw dropping. And, when you add deep-rooted soul and conviction, the result can change lives. Music is that powerful. That's what we're about.

But, it's a battle. A battle for exposure. A battle for attention. A battle for visibility. A battle for sales. A battle for bucks (Can we talk streaming income!!??). And, a battle for truth. The casualties of these battles are many and often legendary.

I have been in the music business for over forty years, as a producer, record executive, record company owner as well as a concert and festival producer. Over the course of time, I've collected the truths, lies, stories, anecdotes and a tapestry of every little musical bit that put a smile on my face. This collection is a celebration of vignettes, conundrums, one-liners, embarrassments, scars and self-assessments.

Our business is filled with artistic people and with creativity comes insecurity. My role as a producer is to encourage, and in the pursuit of capturing an emotional performance, glibly gloss over obvious inadequacies. We tell our artists how bad they are by telling them how good they are. Trust me, it's an art.

If you think that many of the falsehoods you are about to read are the epic truths of our business, then like me, you have been in this business way too long.

If you think that some of the nonsense you are about to read is especially cruel, harsh or too brutal, then you haven't been in the business long enough.

This book is about laughter. At one's self. At our music community. At the world-at-large—those disrespectful bastards.

Is This You?

"Singers and Musicians are some of the most driven, courageous people on the face of the earth. They deal with more day-to-day rejection in one year than most people do in a lifetime.

Every day, they face the financial challenge of living a freelance lifestyle, the disrespect of people who think they should get real jobs, and their own fear that they'll never work again.

Every day, they have to ignore the possibility that the vision they have dedicated their lives to is a pipe dream. With every note, they stretch themselves, emotionally and physically, risking criticism and judgment.

With every passing year, many of them watch as the other people their age achieve the predictable milestones of normal life—the car, the family, the house, the nest egg.

Why? Because musicians and singers are willing to give their entire lives to a moment—to that melody, that lyric, that chord, or that interpretation that will stir the audience's soul.

Singers and Musicians are beings who have tasted life's nectar in that crystal moment when they poured out their creative spirit and touched another's heart. In that instant, they were as close to magic, God, and perfection as anyone could ever be.

And in their own hearts, they know that to dedicate oneself to that moment is worth a thousand lifetimes."—David Ackert (L.A. Times)

If this is you, read on. You need this. It may be the only way you can survive the "truth."

Jeffrey Weber
June, 2019

Gustafsson:

I finally gave a listen to those LPs and the CD you sent me, of your own saxophone playing and some Swedish modern jazz.

I gotta tell you, on the cover of the CD of your sax playing, which is black and has no text on it, I wrote in large block letters, in silver ink, "Torturing the saxophone –Gustafsson."

I just totally fail to find anything enjoyable about this, or to see what this has to do with music, as I understand it, or what in God's name is going on in your head that you would want to make such noises on a musical instrument.

Quite frankly, I was kind of shocked at what a negative, unpleasant experience it was, listening to it. I had to take it off long before it reached the end. I just don't get it. I don't understand what this is about.

You actually go on TOUR with that stuff. Wow. People actually… sit… and… LISTEN… to that. I mean, they voluntarily go to the place, maybe even PAY… PAY to hear that stuff. And then they sit there, quietly, politely… and LISTEN. Unbelievable. I should go myself sometime and see this. Witness it with my own eyes.

I don't say these things with the intention to insult you. You seem to be a perfectly nice, civilized guy with a good sense of humor. I am speaking the plain truth of my reaction to the records and the CD you sent. That this noise could give anyone any aesthetic pleasure is beyond my comprehension, truly.

Is this the logical end of improvisational music? Is this where it ends up? Where does it go from this point? Is there any audience for this "free jazz" besides other guys who play it and maybe their wives who must patiently endure it?

I just don't get it. Am I too un-hip? Am I a square from Delaware? A hick from Battle Crick? A shmuck from Keokuck?

R. Crumb

ConunDrum 1

People are willing to pay $5.00 for a cup of coffee that:
- Cost pennies to make
- Takes minutes to prepare
- Is gone forever after one use

Yet...
Millions of people won't pay $1.00 for a song they like that:
- Cost thousands to record
- Can be used over and over again
- Took years of practice
- And lasts a lifetime

ConunDrum 2

Led Zeppelin—1975
    If the sun refused to shine,
    I would still be loving you.
    When mountains crumble to the sea,
    There would still be you and me.
    Kind woman, I give you my all,
    Kind woman, nothing more.

Nicki Minaj—2012
    You a stupid hoe,
    You a, you a stupid hoe,
    You a stupid hoe,
    You a stupid hoe,
    You a stupid hoe, (yeah)
    You a, you a stupid hoe,
    You a stupid hoe,
    You a, you a stupid hoe (stupid, stupid),
    You a stupid hoe (stupid, stupid),
    You a stupid hoe,
    You a, you a stupid hoe (stupid, stupid)

ConunDrum 3

CREATORS!

1 Writer and 1 Producer:
Queen
    Is this the real life?
    Is this just fantasy?
    Caught in a landslide.
    No escape from reality

Open your eyes.
Look up to the skies and see
I'm just a poor boy, I need no sympathy,
Because I'm easy come, easy go.
Little high, little low.
Any way the wind blows doesn't really matter to me, to me
Mama.
I just killed a man.
Put a gun against his head, pulled the trigger
Now he's dead
Mama…life had just begun.
But now I've gone and thrown it all away
Mamaaaaa oooh.
Didn't mean to make you cry.
If I'm not back again this time tomorrow,
Carry on, carry on as if nothing really matters.

6 Writers and 4 producers:

Beyonce

Girls, we run this mother (yeah!)
Girls, we run this mother (yeah!)
Girls, we run this mother (yeah!)
Girls, we run this mother (yeah!)
Who run the world? Girls (girls)
We run this motha? Girls (girls)
Who run the world? Girls (girls)
Who run the world? Girls (girls)
Girls, we run this mother? Girls
Girls, we run this mother? Girls
Girls, we run this mother? Girls
Girls, we run this mother? Girls
Who run the world? Girls (girls)
We run this motha? Girls (girls)
Who run the world? Girls (girls)
Who run the world? Girls (girls)

Conundrum 4

OBLIGATION VS DESIRE

Being a musician today means composing, writing, playing, singing, arranging, recording producing, mixing, mastering, videoing, uploading, designing, promoting, booking, performing, blogging, messaging and filing tax returns.

And all you wanted was some sex…

Conundrum 5

THE INTERNET

Fan to Artist: "No offense, but I downloaded all your music off the Internet."

Artist to Fan: "None taken. I downloaded all your credit card info off the Internet."

Conundrum 6

RADIO (what's left of it…)

Dear Radio Stations,

You do realize there are more than just five songs in the world, right?

14th April, 1970.

A. Klein, Esq.,
Apple Corps Limited,
3 Savile Row,
LONDON, W.1.

Dear Sir,

   In future no one will be allowed to add to or
subtract from a recording of one of my songs without
my permission.

   I had considered orchestrating "The Long and Winding Road"
but I decided against it.   I therefore want it altered
to these specifications:-

   1. Strings, horns, voices and all added noises to be
      reduced in volume.

   2. Vocal and Beatle instrumentation to be brought up
      in volume.

   3. Harp to be removed completely at the end of the
      song and original piano notes to be substituted.

   4. Don't ever do it again.

                         Signed

                         PAUL MCCARTNEY

c.c. Phil Spector
     John Eastman

RSO Records (U.K.) Limited
A Division of the Robert Stigwood Group Ltd.

67 Brook Street London W1Y 1YE England
Telephone 01-629 9121
Cables Stigwood London W1
Telex 264267

Mr. P. Hewson,
10 Cedarwood Road,
Dublin 11

10th May 1979.

Dear Mr. Hewson,

Thank you for submitting your tape of 'U2' to RSO, we have
listened with careful consideration, but feel it is not
suitable for us at present.

We wish you luck with your future career.

Yours sincerely,

W ALEXANDER SINCLAIR

Mr. Alec Head
c/o Media Sound
311 West 57th Street
New York, N.Y. 10019

Dear Alec: RE: MADONNA

I enjoyed listening to Madonna. The production, arrangements and
she are very strong. The direction is a good one, in my opinion. The
only thing missing from this project is the material. I liked "I Want
You", "Get Up" and "High Society", but I did not like "Love On The Run"
at all. I do not feel that she is ready yet, but I do hear the basis for
a strong artist. I will pass for now, but I will wait for more.

Good luck and thank you for thinking of me.

Best regards,

Jimmy Ienner
President

MURRAY HILL 8-8800   CABLE ADDRESS: ASCAP, NEW YORK

AMERICAN SOCIETY OF COMPOSERS, AUTHORS AND PUBLISHERS
575 MADISON AVENUE
NEW YORK 22, N.Y.

March 27th, 1957

Mr. Henry N. Mancini
Northridge Music Co.
17947 Osborne Street
Northridge, California

Dear Mr. Mancini:

  The Membership Committee regrets to inform you that it does not find the present activity of your catalogue to be sufficient to warrant your election to membership and that it is obliged to return your application.

  You will understand that this step is in no wise a reflection upon your work. However, we find that, at this time, the works lack revenue-producing possibilities. If, at any time, you produce additional works, or have reason to believe that your present works are being generally performed by our licensees, we shall be glad to have you re-submit your application. It will not be necessary for you to fill out a new application blank; simply send us the old one, listing any additional works you may have produced.

  With sincere regrets, and in the hope that we may at a later date number you among our members, I am

          Sincerely yours,

         AMERICAN SOCIETY OF COMPOSERS,
          AUTHORS AND PUBLISHERS,

         A. Walter Kramer

       A. Walter Kramer, Chairman Pro Tem
         Membership Committee

AWK:pn
Enc.

P. S. Under separate cover, we are returning your music.

FROM THE DESK OF SEAN CONNERY

December 11, 1998

Mr. Stephen P. Jobs
c/o Apple Computers
1 Infinite Loop
Cupertino, California

Mr. Jobs:

I will say this one more time. You do understand English, don't
you? I do not sell my soul for Apple or any other company. I have
no interest in "changing the world" as you suggest. You have
nothing that I need or want. You are a computer salesman — I am
fucking JAMES BOND!

I can think of no quicker way to destroy my career than to appear
in one of your crass adverts. Please do not contact me again.

Best,

Sean Connery

SC: tw

An actual
"letter" to
an attorney
in the music
business...

need we
say more.

July 13, 1981

Dear Jon

Please excuse this form letter but time is of the essence. I have
a Band I want to produce and they are ready. It will be Rock
and Jaz Rock . I need your attorney resumes with
work experience, education background, etc., sent to me. It is long
and Ball is rolling .

Please reply at your earliest convenience.

Very sincerely,

P.S. My above address is:

22

Best Backstage Guest List Ever!

BACK DOOR LIST 6-9
RADIOHEAD

8 - ~~Sean Booth~~ Beastie Boys +guests VIP
8 - Blur +guests VIP
Matthew Caws VIP
Kelly Curtis +1 VIP
George Drakoulias
3 - Fast +2 VIP
2 - Ira Elliot VIP
Shalom Harlow +1 VIP
1 - Lenny Kravitz +1 VIP
Courtney Love +1 VIP
2 - Madonna +1 VIP
14 - Marilyn Manson +7 VIP
Dave Matthews + guests VIP
Mike McCready +1 VIP
Kate Moss +2 VIP
Guy Oseary +1 VIP
3 - Oasis +guests VIP
Brad Pitt +1 VIP
4 - REM +guests VIP
2 - Rick Rubin VIP
2 - Russell Simmins +1 VIP
Jill Sobule +1 VIP
18 - U2 +guests VIP
2 - Amber Valetta +1 VIP
Eddie Vedder +1 VIP
2 - Brigitte Wright +2 VIP

8 - Dan Yates (guests)

. 2 - Rachel Felder (guest of Brigitte Wright)

2 - LAVONNE MUKLOWSKY (Gold Mountain Entertainment - /Beastie Boys

2 - Dean Kyrsty

- Mark Blacknell +2

3 - Paul McGuiness +1

1 - Ghiro - Shane Doyle

BACK DOOR

23

Dear Bill:

Historically, Miles Davis would not be of much interest to you for the Fillmore. However, I believe Miles is well on his way to really breaking out of his jazz bag. All the fantastic reviews in ROLLING STONE and Ralph Gleason's latest articles calling Miles' most recent albums the best he's heard anywhere in a decade have given him tremendous impetus. The "underground" is ready for Miles. His sales have measurably increased and I have finally softened him to play the Fillmore type emporium. I would appreciate it if you could express interest to him. In playing a role as "guest impresario" for Columbia, a bill with The Flock, Taj Mahal and Miles might be a real sleeper for you. No one of them would get that much bread as to make it hard to pay all; further, each appeals to that kind of music buff as to make it possible for all to be enjoyed. Creatively it would be a gigantic coup as each artist is felt to be a potential big artist and each has a growing fanatic following. Well, the rest is in your hands.

Santana, as you know, is unstoppable. Total sales with tape are now over 400,000 and going strong.

Warmest regards,

Clive

P.S. I saw Johnny Winter and Chicago Friday night at Fillmore. The evening was electrically exciting. Chicago was very good and Winter just keeps getting better all the time. The combination of him and his brother Edgar had the capacity house on their feet all night.

Mr. Bill Graham
Fillmore West
1945 Market Street
San Francisco, California

November 17, 1969/ob

bc: Teo Macero

24

Biggest Record Company Lies

The Rejection Letter

The Ultimate Record Company Lie
(Here's an actual letter!)

"We find that most submissions we pass on simply lack musical distinction and vision, or quality songwriting. Other times, the vocalist is not unique or mature enough as of yet. Often, we hear music which is too similar to current recording artists, or we hear perfectly good music but with little commercial prospect. Sometimes the music shows too little creativity in arrangements or sonic stylization. We hope this is of some assistance to you."

1. "You've got a deal."
2. "We love your stuff!"
3. "We have your music right in front of us!"
4. "Sure, we listened to it!"
5. "Of course, we pay royalties!"
6. "That's so last week!"
7. "You're a high priority at this label!"
8. "Of course we'll market and promote your project. How do you think we stay in business?"
9. "We'll get you to open for Kanye or Bono or Kendrick."
10. "We'll fix it in the mix."
11. "I was just getting ready to call you!"
12. "We were just talking about you!"
13. "We lost your jump drive... could you send us another one and include return postage?"
14. "Sure, we'll listen to your material..."

15. "I'll listen to your music tomorrow. "
16. "We'll put you on the guest list."
17. "Pick up your backstage passes at Will Call."
18. "We're getting a definite buzz on your record."
19. "It's hot in the clubs."
20. "Now I know this record seems to be starting off slow at radio, but the three stations we have it on nationally are key."
21. "Digital radio is really humping this cut."
22. "We are going to sell a shitload of this stream!"
23. "What—you didn't get the check?"

Biggest Musician and Singer Lies

1. "Just give me one more... I've got it now."
2. "Just give me one more... I've got it now."
3. "Just give me one more... I've got it now."
4. "Sure, I can read!"
5. "I meant to play it that way."
6. "Metronomes hurt your 'feel'!"
7. "I got the gig but some political BS went down, so they gave it to him."
8. "The drum sounds were huge, but the engineer screwed up the mix."
9. "I'll put you on the guest list."
10. "I wasn't fired; the producer just likes to work with his own people."
11. "I can play that!"
12. "I'm really more of a groove player."
13. "They give me everything for free."
14. "I practice five hours a day."
15. "We hardly used a click track at all."
16. "I'm doing tons of sessions!"
17. "They asked me to do the gig, but the money wasn't happening."
18. "They're going to put me in an ad pretty soon."
19. "I played on the record, but I wasn't credited."

20. "I can write…"
21. "Sure, I know that tune."
22. "My girlfriend is an awesome singer."
23. "We're huge in Japan!"
24. "I've got a beautiful axe at home; I just use this piece of shit for gigs."
25. "They don't give me everything for free."
26. "I never practice."
27. "I played Top-40 for years."
28. "I'll never play Top-40."
29. "We've got a few labels interested in us."
30. "I'm really good friends with him."
31. "The Porsche belongs to the banjo player."
32. "Don't save that… I've got a better solo than that."
33. "Sorry I'm late guys… I couldn't find a parking place."
34. "I just got finished recording with…"
35. "Yeah… I just came off the road with…"
36. "You can fix it in the mix."
37. "You're lucky. Those are the only two days I'm available this month."

Biggest Producer Lies

1. "You. Sound. Amazing!"
2. "That was great! You nailed it!"
3. "You wrote that?"
4. (To a songwriter) "Sorry man… we didn't record your song, but we wanted you to know it was the best song we didn't use!"
5. "Our budget is so small, we can't pay you what you're really worth. We're really sorry… how about ¾ scale and you do your own cartage? (Think of the exposure your name will receive once the single drops!)
6. "We need to do one more take… the engineer screwed up."
7. "We'll be finished by noon."
8. "I'll call you next week… really!"
9. "Don't worry… I'll fix it in the mix."
10. "You were the only one we called for this."
11. "That's close enough for jazz."
12. "I really dig your playing. You're going to do all my sessions from now on."
13. "It's not what you play; it's what you don't play that counts." (This one's not a lie.)
14. "Perfect, but let's do it one more time- just to have a safety.
15. "Your material is fabulous!"
16. "What a voice!"
17. "What—you didn't get the check?"

Lies From The Road

1. "The booking is definite."
2. "Your check's in the mail."
3. "This is the best weed you've ever scored."
4. "The show starts at 8."
5. "My agent will take care of it."
6. "I'm sure it will work."
7. "Your tickets are at the door."
8. "It sounds in tune to me."
9. "Sure, it sounds fine at the back of the hall."
10. "I know your mic is on."
11. "I checked it myself."
12. "The roadie took care of it."
13. "She'll be backstage after the show waiting for you."
14. "Yes, the spotlight was on you during your solo."
15. "The monitor mix sounds just like the house mix."
16. "It's the hottest pickup I could get."
17. "The club will provide the PA and lights."
18. "I really love the band."
19. "We'll have it ready by tonight."
20. "We'll have lunch sometime."
21. "If it breaks, we'll fix it for free."
22. "We'll let you know."
23. "I had nothing to do with your marriage breaking up."
24. "The place was packed."
25. "We'll have you back next week."
26. "Don't worry, you'll be the headliner."
27. "It's on the truck."
28. "My last band had a record deal, but we broke up before recording the album."
29. "Someone will be there early to let you in."

30. "I've only been playing for a year."
31. "I've been playing for 20 years."
32. "We'll have flyers printed tomorrow."
33. "I'm with the band."
34. "I'm with the record company."
35. "The band drinks for free."
36. "You'll get your cut tonight."
37. "We'll supply someone for the door."
38. "You'll have no problem fitting that bass cabinet in the trunk of your car."
39. "There'll be lots of roadies when you get there."
40. "It's totally compatible with your current software."
41. "You'll have plenty of time for a soundcheck."
42. "This is one of Jimi's old Strats."
43. "We'll definitely come to the gig."
44. "You can depend on me."
45. "Free parking for everyone in the band."
46. "Your comps are at Will-Call."
47. "What—you didn't get the check?"
48. "Trust me."

Recording Studio Rules of Etiquette

1. Shut your mouth.
2. Do not touch anything.
3. Check if engineer requires a fresh beverage upon entry.
4. Do not intercept any hot girls that approach the studio control room. They are not here to talk to you.
5. If you have any questions, refer to Rule # 1.
6. If you have any questions about Rule # 1, refer to Rule # 7.
7. Get out.

Not bad, fellers. Let's do one more take, with more emphasis on tone, harmony, melody, rhythm, composition, lyrics, musicianship, tempo, and originality.

13 THINGS MUSICIANS ARE SICK OF HEARING AT THE DINNER TABLE!

1. So, are you still doing that music thing?
2. When are we going to hear you on the radio?
3. Hey, my neighbor's kid plays guitar. Seriously, he's really good. You should have him play with you.
4. Sing something.
5. Did you hear the Nelson's daughter is getting married this summer? Maybe you could play at her wedding. I think they're on a tight budget so that could just be your gift. By the way, do you think you'll ever tie the knot? Are you seeing anyone?
6. So, what else do you do for work? I mean, like, during the day.
7. Have you tried out for *The Voice* yet?
8. Did you hear that cousin Jason is going to be having a baby? When are you gonna get on that?
9. Well, we should probably put the family reunion on the calendar now because Jessica always has her music stuff on the weekends.
10. Have you heard that new Taylor Swift song? Why don't you sing more Taylor Swift?
11. Hey, when you open for someone big, you should tell me and I'll come see you.
12. Can you put me on the guest list?
13. Your life always seems so interesting and fun. I wish I had fewer responsibilities.

Relationship Calculator

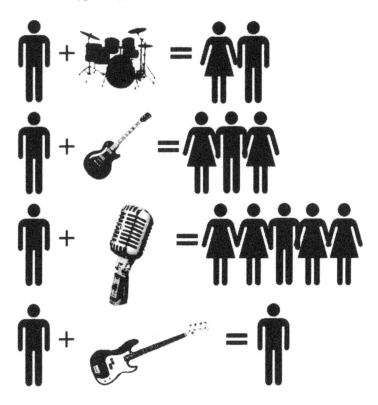

Be a bassist.   Expectation.

Reality.

Dirty Little Truths We Love

Record company executive responding to an artist's attorney's plea for fairness in a clause of the contract: "I'll be Goddamned before I'll commit to being equitable!" (A true story by the way!)

An artist called his A&R guy to find out his response to the artist's latest song submission for his next album. "Well," the artist said, "What do you think?" The A&R guy says, "I don't know- I'm the only one who's heard it."

I Know You!

A man in a hot air balloon realized he was lost. He reduced his altitude and spotted someone below. He descended a bit and shouted "Excuse me, can you help me? I promised a friend I would meet him an hour ago, but I don't know where I am."

The man below replied, "You're in a hot air balloon hovering approximately 30 feet above the ground. You're between 40 and 41 degrees north latitude and between 59 and 60 degrees west longitude."

"You must be a Record Producer," said the balloonist. "I am," replied the man, "How did you know?" "Well," answered the balloonist, "Everything you told me is probably correct, but I've no idea what to make of the information, and I'm still lost. Frankly you've not been much help at all. If anything, you've delayed my trip."

The Producer responded, "You must be an A&R executive." "I am," replied the balloonist, "But, how did you know?" "Well", said the Producer, "You don't know where you are or where you are going. You have risen to where you are due to a large quantity of hot air. You made a promise which you've no idea how to keep, and you expect people beneath you to solve your problems. The fact is you are in exactly the same position you were in before we met, but somehow, it's my fault."

What did the record company executive say as he was leaving the office on Tuesday afternoon? "Have a nice weekend."

Two old retired Jewish musicians sitting on a park bench. First guy: "Oy..." Second guy: "I'm hip."

A visitor to Israel attended a recital and concert at the Moscovitz Auditorium. He was quite impressed with the architecture and the acoustics. He inquired of the tour guide, "Is this magnificent auditorium named after Chaim Moscovitz, the famous Talmudic scholar?" "No," replied the guide. "It's named after Sam Moscovitz, the writer." "Never heard of him. What did he write?" "A check," replied the guide.

You will never find anybody who can give you a clear and compelling reason why instrumental parts are written in transposed pitch. (Especially trumpet parts in E.)

People who feel the need to tell you that they have perfect pitch are telling you that their sense of relative pitch is defective.

The most valuable function performed by a Wagnerian opera is its ability to drown out a rock concert.

You should never say anything to a sideman that even remotely sounds like a compliment unless you are prepared to pay double scale.

A string sample saved is worthless.

Wynton Marsalis can hold all the Jazz Concerts he wants. Billions of years from now, when Earth is hurtling toward the Sun and there is nothing left alive on the planet except a few microorganisms, the microorganisms will still prefer Yanni.

The most powerful force in the universe is Andrew Lloyd Webber.

The one thing that unites all non-musicians, regardless of age, gender, religion, economic status, or ethnic background, is that, deep down inside they all have below-average musical taste.

There comes a time when you should stop expecting other people to make a big deal about your musical talent. That time is age 11.

There is a very fine line between "arranging" and "mental illness."

People who want you to listen to their music almost never want to listen to yours.

At least once per year, Hans Zimmer will become very excited and announce that: (1) His producers loved the first theme he played for them; (2) They loved the second theme even more than the first; (3) He has never composed anything they didn't love.

There apparently exists, somewhere in Los Angeles, a computer that generates music for television dramas. When TV composers need a new dramatic cue, they turn on this computer; after sorting through millions of possible musical themes, it spits out, "ONE LONG LOW SCARY NOTE ON A SYNTHESIZER," and this becomes the cue. The next time they need a cue, the computer spits out, "TWO LONG SCARY NOTES ON A SYNTHESIZER." And so on, ad infinitum. We need to locate this computer and destroy it with hammers—along with TV producers and entertainment lawyers.

If you had to identify, in one word, the reason composers have not achieved, and never will achieve their full potential, that word would be "copyists."

The main accomplishment of Disney Studios was the film "Fantasia" in which they ripped-off Stravinsky's "Rite of Spring" by paying his agent $2,500, of which Stravinsky received $500.

The value of a composer's agent is to convince the producer that using a music-cue library would not be cheaper than hiring a composer.

If there really is a Devil who is out to destroy the universe by means of vile conspiracies, and if God decides to deliver this message to humanity, He will not use, as His messenger—Oliver Stone. But John Williams will write the score.

You should not confuse your lack of musical talent with your inferiority complex.

No group singer is normal.

Best Laid Plans...

A musician who's spent his whole life trying to break into the big time is feeling very depressed. Every single record company in the country has turned him down, and no one seems to recognize his unique genius other than his Mum.

So, he decides to top himself, and dreams up an ingenious plan to get back at all the institutions that have rejected him all his life. He goes into a recording studio and tells the engineer to record exactly what he says, and then copy it onto 1,000 CDs, and send them out to all the record execs in the country.

He goes into the vocal booth, the red light comes on, and he begins: "This is a message to all you sycophantic, talentless bastards who've ignored me all these years. I dedicated my life to writing beautiful, emotive, soul-touching music, and all you do is bin my CDs and sign pretty-boy bands and slutty chick singers. Well, I've taken all I can of your puerile, shallow industry, and it's YOU who have driven me to it!!! Bye-bye, murderers of Art!!"

With that, he pulled out a gun and sprayed his brains all over the studio wall.

The recording engineer glanced up and said "... Yep, okay—that's fine for level. Wanna go for a take?"

One place we played had a fire department sign on the wall that declared: "OCCUPANCY OF THESE PREMISES BY OVER 120 PEOPLE IS UNLAWFUL." Someone had penciled neatly underneath: "AND UNLIKELY."

A movie producer who is suddenly nice to you is not really a nice person. It means he is thinking about hiring another composer, probably John Williams.

No matter what happens at a recording session (for example, the players shout "Bravo" and applaud) somebody will still find something wrong with your music, and the producer will begin to have doubts. Serious doubts.

When musical problems in a film arise and things look bad, there is always one individual who perceives a solution and is willing to take command. Very often, that individual is the producer's brother-in-law. He is a (budding) composer.

Your friends love you, even if you are tone-deaf.

Nobody cares if you can't compose music well. You are certain to succeed if you suck up to the right person.

Dirty Little Truths...Musicians

The stages of a musician's life:
1. Who is ____?
2. Get me ____.
3. Get me someone who sounds like ____.
4. Get me a young ____.
5. Who is ____?

Little Johnny went up to his mother and said, "When I grow up, I want to be a musician!" His mother said, "Johnny, you can't do both."

What's the first thing a musician says at work?
"Would you like fries with that?"

What do you call a musician whose girlfriend leaves him?
Homeless.

What would a musician do if he won a million dollars?
Continue to play gigs until the money ran out.

Why do musicians have to be awake by six o'clock?
Because most shops close by six-thirty.

There were two people walking down the street. One was a musician. The other didn't have any money either.

Micheal Caine goes up to Milton Berle during a party and asks, "What kind of cigar are you smoking there?" "It's a Lawrence Welk." says Milton. "What's a Lawrence Welk?" Micheal asks.

Milton says "It's a piece of crap with a band wrapped around it."

Bar Notes

C, E-flat and G go into a bar. The bartender says, "Sorry, we don't serve minors," and E-flat leaves. C and G have an open fifth between them and after a few drinks, G is out flat. F comes in and tries to augment the situation, but is not sharp enough. D comes into the bar and heads straight for the bathroom saying, "Excuse me, I'll just be a second."

A comes into the bar, but the bartender is not convinced that this relative of C is not a minor and sends him out. Then the bartender notices a B-flat hiding at the end of the bar and shouts "Get out now. You're the seventh minor I've found in this bar tonight."

Next night, E-flat, not easily deflated, comes into the bar in a 3-piece suit with nicely shined shoes. The bartender (who used to have a nice corporate job until his company downsized) says: "You're looking pretty sharp tonight. Come on in. This could be a major development." And in fact, E-flat takes off his suit and everything else and stands there au naturel. Eventually, C, who had passed out under the bar the night before, begins to sober up and realizes in horror that he's under a rest.

So, C goes to trial, is convicted of contributing to the diminution of a minor and sentenced to 10 years of DS without Coda at an up-scale correctional facility. The conviction is overturned on appeal, however, and C is found innocent of any wrongdoing, even accidental, and that all accusations to the contrary are bassless.

The bartender decides, however, that since he's only had tenor so patrons, the soprano out in the bathroom and everything has become alto much treble, he needs a rest and closes the bar.

Schubert's Productivity

A company chairman was given a ticket for the performance of Schubert's Unfinished Symphony. Since he was unable to go, he passed the invitation to the Quality Assurance Manager. The next morning the chairman asked him how he enjoyed it, and instead if a few plausible observations, he was handed a memorandum which read as follows:

1. For a considerable period, the oboe players had nothing to do. Their number should be reduced, and their work spread over the whole orchestra, thus avoiding peaks of inactivity.
2. All twelve violins were playing identical notes. This seems an unnecessary duplication, and the staff of this section should be drastically cut. If a large volume of sound is really required, this could be easily obtained through the use of an amplifier.
3. Much effort was involved in playing demi-semiquavers. This seems an excessive refinement, and it is recommended that all notes should be rounded up to the nearest semiquaver. If this were done, it would be possible to use trainees instead of craftsmen.
4. No useful purpose is served by repeating, with horns, the passage that has already been handled by the strings. If all such redundant passages were eliminated, the concert could be reduced from two hours to twenty minutes.

In light of the above, one can only conclude that had Schubert given attention to these matters, he probably would have had the time to finish his symphony.

New Musician's Casual Contract and Rider

Dear Client:

Thank you for engaging _____ (insert ensemble's name here).

Because we know better than you, please, don't tell us what to do, play, wear, or bring. Please, just simply pay us what we ask, and please forgo all the tedious nickel-and-diming you always try to get away with. (You know who you are!)

We want four (4) COMFORTABLE chairs; not folding metal chairs, not splintery ones, and not those cane chairs where the seat is about to fall through.

Preferably padded. No, MUST be padded.

We will not play outside, so don't ask.

We want to be fed well. The same food your 200 guests eat. What are four more meals, really?

We will not eat sandwiches. Especially not sandwiches on white bread.

And we want to eat at a table. Is that too much to ask? We are not "the help" so please do not treat us that poorly!

Before the engagement, please do not call us. Once we have been hired, that's it...you don't need to talk to us for any other reason.

Please do not call other bands trying to compare prices. We all cost the same. Incidentally, we all wear the same clothes, play the same arrangements, and hire the same people, so it really makes no difference.

Do not make requests for music we don't have. It's just way too much of a pain to cater to your tiny needs. Find a new favorite song. No Andrew Lloyd Webber! Period!!

No song will be transposed down a half-step so your cousin Jeannie can sing it during your candle lighting ceremony. She's not a very good singer anyway.

Forget about The Bride Cuts the Cake, The Hokey Pokey, Alley Cat, The Chicken Dance, etc. These are juvenile songs, we are artists, and we will not degrade ourselves. Furthermore, there is no reason for you to act stupid in front of us.

The garter and bouquet are OK, but do not allow children less than 18 years of age to participate (or 12 years old in Arkansas, Alabama and Mississippi).

Do not allow young children to make requests. The wretched little imps are not as cute as you think they are, and nobody else wants to hear their crummy tunes anyhow.

Thank you for using us, and DO call again!

Sincerely,

What does a musician look for in a wife? Two jobs.

Three musicians walk down the street. If you shot and killed one of them on the spot, how many would be left? One - because the other two will not stay to ask questions.

So, a guy goes to a shrink and says, "Jeez, I feel like killing myself! My life is horrible, worthless!" Shrink says, "Well, let's investigate. What do you do for a living?" Guy says, "I work with the circus." Shrink says, "Well that must be exciting, with lots of travel. So, what do you do with the circus?" Guy says. "I give the elephants enemas. God it's awful! Six elephants a day, by the end of the day, I'm totally covered with it." Shrink says, "Well, this doesn't seem like a hard problem to solve. Just quit your job!" Guy says, "What? And get out of show business?" (For all the musicians who play the clubs.)

What do music and a banana peel have in common? If you don't C sharp, you'll B flat.

What did the 'Deadhead' say when he ran out of pot? "Wow man! This band really does suck!"

Newspaper headline after the death of Jerry Garcia: "Dead Head Head Dead"

A guy walks into the doctor's office and says, "Doc, I haven't had a bowel movement in a week!" The doctor gives him a prescription for a mild laxative and tells him, "If it doesn't work, let me know." A week later the guy is back: "Doc, still no movement!" The doctor says, "Hmm, guess you need something stronger," and prescribes a powerful laxative. Still another week later the poor guy is back: "Doc, STILL nothing!" The doctor, worried, says, "We'd better get some more information about you to try to figure out what's going on. What do you do for a living?" "I'm a musician." The doctor looks up and says, "Well, that's it! Here's $10.00. Go get something to eat!"

Dirty Little Truths...Singers

The musical director was describing the chart to the singer: "The first 4 bars are the intro. We do the intro 3 times, but the third bar is in 5/4. The last time through, the intro is rubato.

We then hit the A section. The first two bars are in 4, then there is a bar of 5 and the fourth bar is in 6. The A section plays down twice with the second time being in double time with a decrescendo over the last two bars the second time through.

We then get to the B section, which is the chorus. We play the chorus twice but the second time through we take the last two bars of the A section in tempo."

At this point the singer interrupts the MD: "Say! How can I remember all these changes?" The MD says: "I don't see why you're having a problem... THAT'S THE WAY YOU SANG IT LAST NIGHT!"

A woman walks into a pet store wanting to buy a songbird. As she is walking around, she hears a bird singing beautifully and, as if in a trance, she follows the sound. There in a cage is a cheerful songbird happily singing her little heart out.

A sign beneath the cage reads, "One thousand dollars for the pair." She looks deeper into the cage and way back she sees this other haggard bird with its head down, shaking it from left to right.

The clerk came over and the woman asked "How much for just the songbird?" "I'm sorry. You'll have to buy the pair," says the clerk. The woman says, "But that other bird is so haggard and looks so depressed, and he's hanging his head and shaking it back and forth. This bird is so happy and singing beautifully. Why do I have to buy that other bird?"

The clerk replies, "Because he's the arranger."

A girl singer approaches a pianist in a jazz club and asks if she can sing one tune with the trio. The pianist says sure. The girl singer says, "How about Lush Life in G flat?" The pianist says quizzically, "G flat?" to which the girl singer blurts out, "Oh, I'm sorry, is that too fast?"

What's the first thing a soprano does in the morning?
Gets up and goes home.

What's the next thing a soprano does in the morning?
Looks for her instrument.

What's the difference between a soprano and a Porsche?
Most musicians have never been in a Porsche.

What is the difference between a soprano and a cobra?
One is deadly poisonous, and the other is a reptile.

How do you put a sparkle in a soprano's eye?
Shine a flashlight in her ear.

What's the difference between a singer and a terrorist?
You can negotiate with the terrorist.

If you threw a violist and a soprano off a cliff, which one would hit the ground first?
The violist. The soprano would have stop halfway down to ask directions.

What's the difference between a soprano and a piranha?
The lipstick

What's the difference between a soprano and a pit bull?
The jewelry.

What's the difference between a Wagnerian soprano and the average All-Pro offensive lineman?
Stage makeup

What's the difference between a Wagnerian soprano and a Wagnerian tenor?
About 10 pounds.

How can you tell if a Wagnerian soprano is dead?
The horses seem very relieved.

What do a soprano and a pirate have in common?
They're both murder on the high C's

How is a soprano different from a sewer rat?
Some people actually like sewer rats.

What do you see if you look up a soprano's skirt?
A tenor.

If you took all the tenors in the world and laid them end-to-end, it would be a good idea.

What's the difference between an alto and a tenor?
Tenors don't have hair on their backs.

Where is a tenor's resonance?
Where his brain should be.

What's the definition of a male quartet?
Three men and a tenor.

*"Ladies and gentlemen, sometimes the one you
love falls in love with another, and when that happens, it is very
sad indeed. It happened to me, and I wrote this
song. It's called 'Fuck You, Steve.'"*

A singer is walking down the street and bumps into an A&R guy. They greet each other and the A&R guy says, "It's really great to see you. I'd love to hear your material."

The singer says, "Thank you, I'd love to have you hear it." The A&R guy says, "I'll have my secretary call you and set up an appointment." The singer says, "You're wonderful, I wish I knew ten like you."

Several weeks go by and they meet again in the street. "Oh", says the A&R guy, "how good it is to see you." The singer replies, "You're great, I wish I knew ten like you." The A&R guy says, "I really do want to hear your new work; perhaps I can get you a record contract. I'll have my secretary set up an appointment with you."

Several weeks later they run in to each other again. "Hey," says the A&R guy, "I know my secretary hasn't called you yet, but I will really have her do it because I really want to hear your new work." The singer gushes, "Gee, I wish I knew ten like you."

The A&R guy finally says, "You know, you keep saying you wish you knew ten like me. I don't understand why you say that when I haven't come through for you." The singer says, "I wish I knew ten like you, because I know a hundred like you!"

A vocalist hired a piano player to accompany her at an audition for a nightclub job. After listening to a couple of songs, the owner said, "Can you sing *When Sunny Gets Blue*? It's my favorite song. If you can sing it, you're hired." The singer whispered to the piano player, "I don't know it all the way through." The piano player said, "I know it. Go ahead and start, and I'll prompt you." Reluctantly she began: "When Sunny gets blue…" She looked at the piano player for help. He whispered confidently, "Bbm9…"

How do you tell if a tenor is dead?
The wine bottle is still full and the comics haven't been touched.

Did you hear about the tenor who was so arrogant, the other tenors noticed?

How can you tell when a singer is at your door?
They can't find the key, and don't know when to come in.

How does a young man become a member of a high school chorus?
On the first day of school he turns into the wrong classroom.

What do you call someone who hangs around musicians?
A Vocalist.

What do you call a vocalist with a college degree?
Night manager at McDonalds.

Why can't vocalists have colostomies?
Because they can't find shoes to match the bag.

What would you call a singing group from Tombstone, Arizona?
The OK Chorale.

What's the difference between a puppy and a singer/ songwriter?
Eventually, the puppy stops whining.

At the completion of his solo, the tenor commented, "If I had known I was going to sound this good, I would have practiced more."

Why bury a singer 6 feet under? Because deep down, they are nice people.

What Your Taste In Music Says About You On A Date

It's one of the quintessential (and sometimes dreaded) first questions: "What kind of music are you into?"

There's a reason that most people tend to side-step this question with a deft, "A little bit of everything." It's because your taste in music reveals *a lot* about you to potential partners.

Here's the breakdown:
- AC/DC: If you're a woman, you're the kind of person who lets a guy move in with you after three dates because he's temporarily homeless. If you're a guy, you're temporarily homeless.
- Aerosmith: Your wild days are behind you.
- Ani DiFranco: You're a good communicator. Maybe too good.
- Arcade Fire: You spend the first third of a relationship in a romantic frenzy and the last two trying to justify it.
- The Beastie Boys: You believe that loyalty is rewarded.
- The Beatles: Eh. Who knows?
- Bebel Gilberto: You're going to flutter little kisses all over every inch of your date's body as soon as you get the chance. Also: You're a foodie.
- Beethoven: You're guarded but sensitive.
- Belle and Sebastian: If you hook up, it's gonna get weird.
- Best Coast: You fall in love way too easily, but only for, like, a week.
- Beyonce: You're sweet, but not a pushover.
- Billy Joel: You know *exactly* what you're doing.
- Bob Dylan: You're an asshole, but you don't know it.

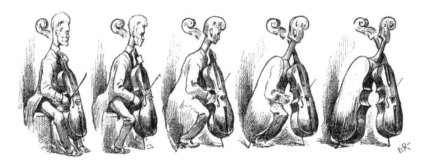

- Bob Seger: It's not your first time around the block.
- Brahms: You're sensitive but guarded.
- Britney Spears: If you're a gay guy or a woman, you're normal. If you're a straight guy, you're trying to get laid.
- Bruce Springsteen: You're a monster in the sack.
- Cat Power: You're already getting over your inevitable break-up.
- Cat Stevens: You had a glorious youth.
- Charles Mingus: You're cool as hell.
- The Clash: You're willing to work for it, but you're kind of pissed that you have to.
- Coldplay: Missionary position only. But lots of kissing and eye contact.
- Cut Copy: You make out in public a lot.
- The Cure: You fall in love WAY too easily.
- Daft Punk: Depends. You're either prone to "raging" in the sense of "partying a lot" or in the sense of "throwing your X-Box controller on the floor and smashing it with your purple Sam Jackson light saber replica."
- David Bowie: You're selective, but slutty.
- Depeche Mode: You're screwed up, but you know it, which actually does help.
- Drake: You're about whatever.
- Eminem: You have emotional problems.
- Fleetwood Mac: You're reasonably well adjusted. Considering.
- Frank Sinatra: It bugs you that people aren't classier these days.

- Gogol Bordello: You sweat a lot and you have a nice smile.
- Green Day: You get upset over nothing all the time, but bounce back quickly.
- Guns N Roses: You're going to have to sex in the bathroom and regret it.
- Hall and Oates: You're not the type to let your wistful nature ruin your good time.
- Insane Clown Posse: You're not the type to let common decency ruin your good time.
- Jack Johnson: Chill and easy going, allowing the relationship to take a natural path (versus rushing into anything).
- Jack Johnson: You *think* you're chill and easygoing, but really, you're just afraid of commitment.
- Jay Z: You don't take any shit. Or at least you know that you're not supposed to.
- Jewel: Um… are you sure this is a *date*?
- Joan Jett: You're going to have sex in the bathroom and not regret it.
- John Coltrane: Deeply introspective.

- John Legend: You have emotional sex.
- John Mayer: You're a virgin.
- Joni Mitchell: You make breakfast in the morning.
- Judas Priest: At some point in your life, you've sniffed a little glue.
- Justin Timberlake: You seem really lame at first, then turn out to be awesome.
- Kanye West: You're kinda mean. In a hot way.
- Kid Cudi: No one understands you. But it's not that big a deal.

- Lady Gaga: You're sort of obnoxious, but people can't help but like you.
- LCD Soundsystem: You're not the type to let your strong sense of irony ruin your good time.
- Led Zeppelin: If you're a woman, you're hot. If you're a guy, you're average.
- Leonard Cohen: You're the kind of person that people get obsessed with for years. Too bad you're too depressed to appreciate it.

- Lil' Kim: You're really kinky.
- Lil' Wayne: You're crazy. And kind of awesome.
- Lupe Fiasco: You wrestle with moral dilemmas but never at the expense of your chill demeanor.
- Madonna: You're kind of bratty, but you're hot enough to pull it off.
- Mandy Moore: You have American Girl dolls. Plural.
- Miles Davis: Introspective.
- Mos Def: You're straightforward.
- The Mountain Goats: You're very serious about your feelings.
- Mozart: Smartypants.
- My Chemical Romance: You're not so much looking for a boyfriend or girlfriend as someone to share a "fuckyeahsuperheroeskissing" Tumblr with.
- Nickelback: You have low self-esteem and bad tattoos. But, god bless you.
- Nicki Minaj: You're awesome. And kind of crazy.
- Nine Inch Nails: You're kinky and have lots of angry sex.
- Nirvana: You're angry and hurt.
- No Doubt: If you're a girl, you're a confident person, but you know what it's like to get treated like crap. If you're guy, you're just trying to get laid.
- Oasis: You're the kind of person who does things they're not supposed to do. Like liking Oasis.

- Panda Blood: You made that up to see if your date would pretend to have heard of them.
- Paul Simon: You're sincerely insightful about your relationship issues, but in the end, you decide that it's not your fault.
- Peaches: If you're not getting a hand-job under the table right now, it's because you're giving one.
- Peter Gabriel: Every relationship is a coming-of-age epic of which you are the star.
- Pink Floyd: Your alcohol/substance use prevented you from making it to the date, but the hours spent in heavy contemplation left you a better person. For now.
- The Pixies: Relax. You're cool.
- Prince: You're a little weird, but you make up for it by being a total sex machine.
- Queen: You love with the heart of a warrior.
- Radiohead: You're angry and hurt. But you're open to getting some professional help.
- The Ramones: Unless you're over 40, you're trying to be cool.
- Red Hot Chili Peppers: You're not super-interesting, but you're nice enough and you're certainly not going anywhere, so…
- Regina Spektor: You might be a perfectly nice person, but you're kind of annoying.
- R.E.M.: You've got a big heart.
- Rihanna: You're hot.
- Rod Stewart: You're gross.
- The Rolling Stones: You're hot.
- Rush: You're a man. And a nerdy one at that.
- The Shins: You either really liked "Garden State," or have a giant chip on your shoulder about how people only like The Shins because of "Garden State."
- The Smiths: It's doomed every time, but it always takes a beautiful, long while to figure that out.
- Stevie Wonder: You're husband/wife material.
- Stravinsky: You're romantic. Sometimes aggressively so.

- The Strokes: You're not really an asshole, you just act like it sometimes.
- The Talking Heads: You're a good person.
- Thelonious Monk: You're cool as hell. Even though you're wearing mismatched socks.
- Tool: You're either really smart or really dumb.
- Tori Amos: You cry during sex and get *real quiet* after.
- T-Rex: You're an asshole.
- TV on the Radio: You care. Deeply. Even if you act like you don't.
- U2: You're very loving, but prone to fits of irritating self-righteousness.
- Vampire Weekend: You're about being about whatever.
- Van Morrison: You're a romantic. Possibly with a slight drinking problem.
- Weezer: Awkward. And proud of it.
- The White Stripes: You're kind of kinky.
- The Who: You're a generally open, curious person, but you get really riled up when people cut in front of you in line and stuff.
- Wilco: You'll make an excellent life-partner.

HOW To Be MePioCre

"I can't even follow him on Twitter."

1. Avoid transcribing at all costs
    *   Convince yourself that great players never transcribed and choose to believe that they invented everything they played, straight from their own mind. When teachers or friends suggest that you transcribe, act like you're above it and reply, "I'm looking to do my own thing."
    *   Perhaps if you're in music school though, you're required to transcribe for an assignment. Just try to write the notes down on paper as quickly as possible. That way you'll avoid learning any of the language or concepts in the solo, while still being able to talk about what the soloist is doing.

- If you really feel the urge to know what someone is playing, search frantically for a transcription of the solo. If you can't find it online, you could always purchase a book of transcriptions. These are great tools to help you avoid transcribing all together, ensuring you never rise above mediocre.

2. Always learn tunes from fake books
   - Act like it's impossible to learn tunes off records. Argue that you must learn the authoritative version of the tune: the one that's written down on a lead sheet. If by chance someone tells you you're playing a wrong chord, pull out your fake book and show them what the real changes are. That will teach them!

3. Don't ever learn lines
   - Take the attitude that learning lines that your heroes played is copying and unoriginal. You know for a fact that the professionals never did this; they learned their scales and arpeggios and rearranged the notes on the spot into beautiful melodies.

4. Don't ever learn anything in all keys
   - One key is good enough. Really, who plays rhythm changes in anything other than Bb?

5. Don't waste your time on easy tunes
   - Never waste your time with easy tunes. Easy tunes are for wimps. These include blues, rhythm changes, and most standards. The only tunes worth spending any time on are Monk, Joe Henderson, and Wayne Shorter tunes, so you should jump straight to these. That way when you're at a jam session, you can impress everyone because you can almost approximate the melody to "Inner Urge." Don't worry about soloing over it. I mean, the head is hard enough, right?
6. Never play over the original changes
   - If by chance you have to play a standard for a school assignment or some sort of requirement, re-harmonize all the chords so you can barely hear the original changes. Who needs to hear another two-five progression? You don't need to play over another two-five in your life. That's old-hat.
   - If you don't have time to work out the mathematics of your re-harmonization (You wouldn't dare do this by sound. You should base your re-harmonization on theory), superimpose as many things as you can. Write these new changes on the lead sheet to ensure you play them during performance.
7. Ear training. Who needs it?
   - You need to focus on your fingers. Not your ears. Enough said.
8. If you're not getting the results you want, get new equipment
   - You know all your scales and arpeggios. You even wrote down a Coltrane solo once. You've played chorus after chorus with play-along tracks, so the problems couldn't possibly lie with you. Use this reasoning to always blame your equipment. Spend at least an hour a day, preferably more, searching for new mouthpieces or other equipment on Ebay, or trying to figure out what equipment your hero plays on. Know that if you just get the right equipment, you'll be the next Trane.

"We conductors live long because we suck the life out of the orchestra."

9. Work on scales and arpeggios until you're blue in the face
   - You know that the jazz theory model of playing has proved that mastering all your scales and arpeggios results in perfect improvisation. So, keep on truckin'. Eventually, they will magically turn into the half-assed melodies you've always dreamed of.
   - When you don't seem to be able to get through a two-five, learn a new scale choice so you feel like you're working towards your goal. When this new scale doesn't help you, rave about how it is helping you, and that you've finally found the sound you've been after.

10. Only do the minimum amount of work
    - Just do the bare minimum. Your goal is to not play wrong notes. That's it. If you get through a whole chorus with no wrong notes, you're killin' it!! All your work should go into this one goal because that's what matters: no wrong notes.

11. Don't worry about chord progressions
    - Chord progressions are just suggestions. They're just written symbols after-all. It's not like they are sounds.

Instead of trying to understand the progression, just look for general tonality, then find the major scale that fits over it and go to town!!!

12. Never ever play with a metronome
   - You're not going to perform with a metronome, so why practice with one? If your teacher makes you play with one, avoid playing with it on 2 and 4, as that might improve your time-feel above mediocre.

13. Always use play-alongs
   - Why use recordings of your heroes when the soloist is in the way all the time?! Purchase every play-along you can and make them the only thing you practice. Open the book, put the back-up track on and see what comes out. You are your own hero. Don't let anyone on the recording get in your way. Play chorus after chorus, close your eyes, and move your fingers. Eventually something great has to come out, right?

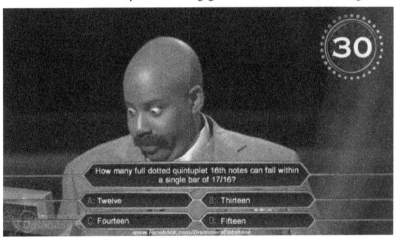

14. Learn as many tunes as you can
   - You know that the more tunes you learn the better because then when you go to a jam session, you won't feel dumb when you don't know a tune. Who cares how you sound on it, as long as you know it and someone else doesn't. Make sure to make fun of the person who doesn't know the tune by saying, "Really, you don't know this tune?"

- And your definition of learning is memorizing the melody and the chord sequence on the lead sheet. That should be enough to get you to your goal of not playing wrong notes, and if by chance you hit a few wrong ones, just blame it on the fact that you love playing "outside."
- You can be mediocre!
- Good news! With little effort, you can become mediocre! If this list reads like your modus operandi, then you can be sure, you'll reach your goal of playing mediocre in no time. Don't change a thing. Avoid anyone who suggests you do anything different than what you're currently doing and seek others who feel the same way you do about everything. You're on the path of mediocrity and loving it, so keep going!

15. The Mediocre Bibles

Little Bits

Tonight's Rock Concert Ticket Special: Buy one ticket for the price of two and receive a second ticket ABSOLUTELY FREE!

Worth A Try
Maybe if we over-paid our teachers and under-paid our Pop artists there would be better education and less bad music.

"Yeah, our first album went vinyl."

If you're wearing a t-shirt of a band you've never heard of—SHAME ON YOU!

If you were a rock band you would be Van Failin.

Which way?
Highway to Hell or Stairway to Heaven?

After every bath, my baby needs a soft towel and heavy metal.

Geology Quiz
Question: Name the three types of rock.
Answer: 1. Classic 2. Punk 3. Hard

Who's Complaining?
I used to suffer alone…in silence. Now, through music, I can cause many others to suffer.

A Life Changer
To all of you who still think that music can't change lives, I just want to say…it's certainly screwed up mine!

"I do this for the money," said no musician, EVER!

The New Math
What concert costs 45 cents?
50 Cent featuring Nickleback.

Workplace Therapy
"They say music can make employees more productive. Get back to work or I'll start singing!"

Dreamin'
One day I'll find that special someone who gets just how awesome my record collection really is.

Too Much Of A Good Thing
Son visits father's enormous, wall-to-wall music collection filled with thousands and thousands of albums, 45s and CDs. "Wow Dad," he marvels, "You have almost as much music in here as I have in my iPod!"

Works Every Time

Disc Jockey to his listening audience: "Let me ruin your favorite song by playing it fifteen times a day, seven days a week!"

The Price Is Right!

To all who moan about the price of musicians: A guy calls the musicians' union to get a quote on a six-piece band for a wedding. The representative says, "Off the top of my head, about $2,000. The guy says, What!!?? For music??" The representative responds, "I'll tell you what. Call the plumbers' union and ask for six plumbers to work from six p.m. until midnight on a Saturday night. Whatever they charge you, the band will work for half."

The Tell

I was in China producing a TV/CD project for EMI and the communist party of China. After a long rehearsal, I was at a bar in Shanghai when some cat just dropped a bag of blow on the table. I asked him why and he said he knew we were musicians. I asked him what gave us away and he said, "Every other word you say is mutherfucker!" (True story!)

Heavenly Prayer

Dear Lord,

If we give you Justin Bieber and Miley Cyrus, can we have Muddy Waters and John Lee Hooker back?

Amen.

Ah, Nature

There are only two things dumber than a singer—a turtle and a tree.

To Be Read With A Scottish Accent

What's the difference between Bing Crosby and Walt Disney? Bing sings, Walt Dis'ny.

Long Ago

So, the legend says that the "M" from MTV originally stood for Music…

What You Can Do With A Music Degree
   18% - Teach
   12% - Perform
   8% - Compose
   62% - Die in Poverty

Have You Noticed?
   Bono is somewhat of an anomaly. His band mates seem to like him; it's just the rest of the world that hates him...

   The definition of a Musician: One pissed off girlfriend away from being homeless.

Musician Superfood

The Next Time A Musician Is Asked To Play For Free

Ad:

"We are a small and casual restaurant downtown and we are looking for solo musicians to play in our restaurant to promote their work and sell their music. This is not a daily job, but only for special events, which will eventually turn into a nightly event if we get positive response. More jazz, rock, and smooth type music, around the world and mixed cultural music. Are you interested to promote your work? Please reply back ASAP."

A Musician's Reply:

"Happy New Year! I am a musician with a big house looking for a restaurateur to come to my house to promote his/her restaurant by making dinner for my friends and me. This is not a daily job, but only for special events, which will eventually turn into a nightly event if we get a positive response. More fine dining and exotic meals and mixed ethnic and fusion cuisine. Are you interested to promote your restaurant? Please reply back ASAP."

OR, to put it in concise terms:

Asking a musician to play "for exposure" is like asking a prostitute to turn a trick "for practice."

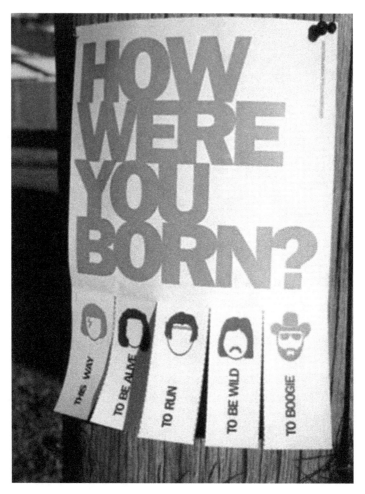

Looking For A Wedding Band

(Actual Craigslist ad that was flagged for removal shortly after posting)

Terrible band needed for sham of a wedding. 11/6. No Pay. As the musician in our family, my shylock of a half-brother and his parsimonious fiancé have passed off to me the job of finding a band for their wedding. I love the kid, but his unique brand of expectant coercion and astonishingly consistent lack of judgment have left me with no recourse but to literally give him what he wants, a band that can "tear up Skynyrd, and won't cost nothin'."

Since they think music is spontaneously generated via voodoo magic by assemblies of self-promoting philanthropists, I am now on a quest to find the best working band interested in "doing it for the exposure."

If you are a serious musician that values your craft and earns a living from performance, you're probably thinking "F**k you. Do you ask your accountant to do your taxes for the exposure." You are not who I am looking for. Thanks for looking.

If, however, you and your unemployable band of pothead hobbyists are enticed by the prospect of a free open bar stocked with the finest of suburban banquet hall well-liquor and an opportunity to run a train on the most whorish collection of self-entitled bridesmaids this side of a Sex In The City marathon, please contact me. There's probably dinner in it for you too, if the starched v****a of a "wedding planner" (bride's bff) can get her 3rd rung caterer to leave a few sandwiches in a storage closet for you at some point in the evening.

What I need from the band:

I don't care if you are an original Icelandic thrash-raga act featuring steam calliope and backwards Armageddon poetry, but I need you to be able to train wreck your way through a few requests.

"Don't Stop Believing." You provide the high notes; we'll provide the smell of wine and cheap perfume.

"Free Bird." Go nuts with the solo. Really. If this evening was a never-ending cascade of sonic punishment hailing down on Tom at blaringly inconsiderate volumes, it would only serve as apropos karmic revenge for afternoons I've spent listening to Jillian chatter about OHMYGODIDON'TCAREWHAT.

"Macarena"/"Electric Slide"/"Chicken Dance." It doesn't matter which one you play, but there has never been a classy party where one of these songs has made an appearance. This will not be a classy party.

Do Not Play:

"Jessie's Girl." I used to play weddings, and if I have to hear this song one more time, I'm going to f**king cut someone.

They said they don't have any preferences for attire, so I'll take that to mean you're ok in a threadbare Megadeth shirt and black jeans.

I will provide the PA (the band and sound system are my wedding present to them).

This is not a joke. Please shoot me an email if this sounds like something you might be interested in.

You're Hired!
(Actual Craigslist Posting)

PRO Bassist Available

Bass player available for PAYING GIGS ONLY. I play G, C, D. If your songs are not in those keys, please transpose them into G. If your song has an Em or Bm or anything off the wall, I will have to sit out that chord. Or, I could learn those notes for $30 each. If you want me to do some fancy stuff like go back and forth between G and D while you hold a G chord, forget it. Minimum $100 per gig within a five-mile radius of 39202. $5 per mile travel charge for anything outside the five-mile radius. Please make sure your gigs are on a JATRAN bus route, or you can pick me up at my place. I have had some previous legal hassles. No gigs within 500 yards of schools, parks or playgrounds.

Ad For Drummer Personally Attacks Previous Drummer

WENATCHEE, WA—While announcing the group's search for a new drummer, an ad posted in a music shop Wednesday by local post-hardcore band Machu Picchu appeared to attack both the character and abilities of its last drummer. "Band seeks drummer who can actually keep the beat and show up to practice without fucking complaining about it all the time," read the flyer, which also stated that candidates should own their own drum kit, not be in any other bands, and not be "the kind of jerk who never helps us move the amps when the show's over but still has the nerve to ask for a ride home." "We need someone who won't sit there playing a bunch of loud fills while we're trying to tune up and then fail to find the fucking two and four when it's time to start the song. And seriously, don't storm off in anger just because Joel says you came in too early." The ad went on to specify that if a potential drummer has a girlfriend, that's fine, but if, "you start missing shows because her parents are visiting and she wants you to go out to dinner with them, then it's time to man up and just tell Cindy to fuck off."

Raising The Bar
(Flyer actually found on telephone pole)

"Tired of watching the Douche with the guitar get the women?
Become that Douche.
Cheap Guitar/Songwriting Lessons
Call Patrick at 659-___-____."

Guitar God Looking for Serious Musicians
(Actual Craigslist posting)

"I am the new guitarist in NH that will bring your band to the top. Need Hendrix? You got it. Need Jimmy Page, Stevie Ray, Clapton? I'm all over that shit. My versatility is incomprehensible to you. I turn from Kirk Hammet to Jerry Garcia on a dime. Hear me play and think you got punched in the balls. I live in Hooksett and sometimes in Manchester. You pick me up. I use a lot of drugs and use them well. I drink scotch, all fucking day. I can play live for 20 hours straight. I own and operate multiple buses. I have been in over 100 fights and have only lost two. (One was because the guy's friend came out with a sword and hacked the shit out of my arms. The other was with the cops.) I also play the bass—in crouch position. I am an exceptional conversationalist, am well versed in 19th—20th century philosophy AND have legal expertise. I abide by an ethical humanist code. I can fix any fucking thing, mechanical and/or electrical. Email me your specs. If you've got what it takes, I will respond."

The Difference Between A Poser and a True Genius

"I'm a creative genius, and there's no other way to word it."

—Kanye West

"I don't consider myself to be the best…and I don't like compliments…they distract me."

—Jimi Hendrix

Are You A Parent Or A Rock Star?

1. Endless hours on the road with too many people in the middle.
2. Your job is to entertain a room full of loud, writhing maniacs.
3. If you do your job well, people ask when you'll produce more.
4. You ask yourself daily: "Am I tripping? Or did I really just see that?"
5. Your name is always shouted, never spoken.
6. Someone is always pulling at your clothes.
7. Groupies follow you to the bathroom.
8. There's a different person in your bed every night. Sometimes even two.
9. At the end of your work-day, you're sweaty and your hair is a mess.
10. Screaming is just part of the job.

"If someday we all go to prison for downloading music, I just hope they segregate us by genre."

Dilemmas

Daughter: "Mom, I think I'm in love with a guitar player."
Mother: "That's ok, honey. They have meds for that now."

Daughter: "Mom, I think I love a drummer."
Mother: "You were always an idiot."

Daughter: "Mom, I think I'm in love with a bass player."
Mother: "That's ok, honey. At least it's not a drummer."

Always Sharomski!

When I was a young boy, my father took me to a concert by Yehudi Menhuin. It was absolutely marvelous, and started in me a lifelong love of the violin.

I first met my business partner, Eyal Ledermann, at a concert given by the teenaged sensation Itzhak Perlman. In the intervening years we've accompanied each other to performances by the greatest virtuosi—Valeri Glava, Augustin Hadelich, Maxim Vengerov, Vadim Repin—we've heard them all.

Early last year, in great excitement, I told Eyal I had secured a pair of tickets to hear Joshua Bell at The Wigmore Hall. "Alas, Moishe," he said, "Sharomski is playing that evening, and so I cannot come."

I was disappointed but no matter, I let someone else have the ticket.

A couple of months later, I acquired with great difficulty a pair of tickets for Anne-Sophie Mutter at The Southbank Centre. Imagine my dismay when once again Eyal declined the opportunity on account of this "Sharomski," who was playing elsewhere that same evening.

Last week, I bought two tickets to a performance by Sarah Chang at The Royal Albert Hall.

And again—"I'm sorry Moishe, but Sharomski . . . "

I lost my temper. Wouldn't you?

"Sharomski! Sharomski! Always Sharomski!"

"Who is this Sharomski? How come you never invite me? Where does he play? What does he play? Tell me Eyal!!!"

He gripped my shoulders, looked me in the eye and quietly said, "Moishe, my friend. I don't know who Sharomski is. I don't know where he plays. I don't know what he plays. I don't even know why he plays.

But whenever he plays, Moishe...I SCHTUPP his WIFE!!!"

Awkward!

There's that awkward moment when you're singing a song you used to sing a lot when you were a kid.........and you suddenly understand the lyrics.

There's that awkward moment when someone in front of you is singing your favorite song but the lyrics are wrong.

Son, someday you will make a girl very happy, for a short period of time. Then, she will leave you and be with new men who are ten times better than you could ever hope to be. These men are called musicians.

"This is the best song ever!!! (Listening to music by yourself)
"It gets better in a minute, I swear!" (Playing music for friends)

Mother to son who is practicing his drums, "That sound… the one between the beats. Practice that for a while."

Piano

Now What?
Pianist Wanted

A man walks into a piano bar at lunchtime, clutching a small ad torn from a newspaper. There's a pretty waitress at the coffee machine.

"I've come about the job," he says without preamble.

"I'm sorry sir, I don't think we're hiring," replies the waitress pleasantly.

"Pianist Wanted" he says, jabbing his finger at the crumpled newspaper clipping.

"Oh, I'm sorry sir, but the manager auditioned yesterday and made his choice already."

"Fuck that!! That's MY job!! Where is the bastard?"

The waitress rushes into the back office and says to her boss, "There's a really aggressive man at the bar. He's come about the audition.

I told him you'd got somebody already but he's not having it. I'm frightened of him sir. Please, would you deal with it?"

The manager goes out to the bar.

"How dare you come barging in here, intimidating my staff? The job's gone. I booked a guy yesterday."

"Can he play?"

"You arrogant so and so," says the manager, "Can YOU?"

"I never thought you'd ask!" replies the man.

He walks briskly to the piano, throws open the lid, slides onto the stool and begins to play.

Ok, so I put the lime
In the coconut. Now what?

Oh man—beautiful beyond beautiful—the sweetest ballad, honey dripping from every note, exquisite yearning harmonies, this cat lays it down so fine it's like time stands still.

He concludes with a cadenza so perfect that it must have been created by almighty god himself, and when the last limpid chord has died away, the manager says, "I've never heard anyone better in my life! You're hired!!!"

The two men quickly discuss terms, shake hands on the deal, and the manager goes to the phone to cancel the other cat.

The waitress seems to have lost her fear. In fact, she seems to have lost her mind. Trembling with ardor, she approaches the musician and says breathlessly, "That was the most beautiful tune I've ever heard—was it yours?"

"Sure was. I write all my own material," he replies.

She leans closer. "What's it called?"

"Screwing Under The Stars While The Moon Lights Up Your Arse." "Now please fuck off."

That same evening, the house is packed, and the manager is anxiously pacing the street outside the premises. The pianist eventually saunters up, forty minutes late.

"Don't you ever do this to me again," yells the manager. "I'm trying to run a business here, goddammit!! You're on!!!"

"Cool daddy-oh," says the musician. "Y'gotta make allowances for genius…"

He takes his place at the piano, and reaches for the microphone.

"Sorry to have kept y'all waiting—heavy traffic. I'd like to start off with a tune of mine. This one's called . . . "Nuts On Your Chin.""

There are audible gasps from one or two of the patrons. Somebody drops a glass.

The musician launches into a blistering neo-bop workout, shredding the keys with frenetic turn-on-a-dime right hand runs, cascading left hand figures punctuated by tone cluster bombs. The crowd goes crazy, whooping, whistling, stamping and yelling. It's pandemonium.

"Thank you thank you—whoa—easy, crew . . . nice, nice . . . okay.

Next one up's a sweet little waltz for a change of pace—hope you like it. This one's called… "Your Pussy's Too Big.""

"Well really—this is too much! You thoroughly disgusting man!" says a woman as she gets up from the table next to the piano. "Come on Raymond—we're leaving," and she drags her protesting companion towards the exit as the pianist begins the number.

Now, round about the third chorus, the musician notices a beautiful woman seated at the table adjacent to the one recently vacated. She's sensational. Classy. Built. Her companion looks bored. But she's digging his playing, hanging on every phrase. When he plays 'out' she thrills to the tension, shivering and arching her back. When he throws in a quote, she gets it and laughs in delight.

Now, to cut a long story short, every number he plays is sublime, and every title he calls is outrageous. But she's really into him, and keen for him to know it.

"Damn, she's so fine, she's giving me the horn," thinks the cat.

He can barely concentrate as he plays the last tune of the set ("Her Dad Don't Dig Me Dickin' His Daughter") to rapturous applause, and leaves the stage, folding his jacket over his arm to hide his throbbing hard-on. But she's gone! Nowhere to be seen!

People are slapping his back, offering him drinks, asking for autographs. He tells them all to fuck off.

Where is she? Finally, he gives up.

"Damn!" he thinks to himself. "I've gotta have a wank!"

He charges into the restroom, bolts a cubicle door, whips out his Johnson and gets to work. He's just reaching the vinegar strokes when he hears the thunderous pounding of fists on the cubicle door. It's the manager.

"Second set!" he hollers.

"Shit! Okay, okay...I'm coming!"

When he returns to the stage, the gorgeous woman is seated alone at the table right next to the piano. Her ankles are slender, her limbs are shapely, her jersey dress clings in all the right places. She's incredible.

All the way through the first number, she's right there. He can smell her perfume. She's driving him crazy. As the final chord dies away, she leans in and says huskily, "Do you know your cock's hanging out and there's jizz dripping on your shoes?"

"Know it?" he replies with a grin. "Baby, I fuckin' WROTE it!!"

All The Motivation You Need
"All right Billy, until your 'staccato' touch improves, we'll be having our piano lessons here at the gas stove."

Request Time
"Thanks, but I don't think I know, 'Here, buy yourself some lessons!'"

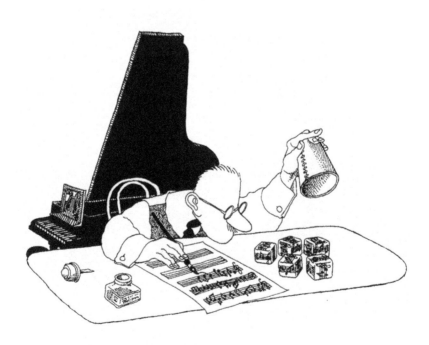

Make a wish

A man walks into a bar and takes from his pocket a miniature piano, which he places on the bar. He then takes from another pocket a 10-inch tall man who promptly sits down at the piano and begins to play. The bartender comes over and is astonished. "Where did you get that little guy and the piano?" he asks. The man replies, "There's a very accommodating genie outside who will grant any wish. There's only one problem..." Without waiting to hear any more, the bartender runs out of the bar. He returns a short time later, surrounded by a huge number of quacking ducks and followed by wave after wave of still more ducks. "What the hell is wrong with the genie?" he asks the man, "I asked him for a million bucks." I started to tell you" the man replies, "The genie has a hearing problem. Do you think I asked for a 10-inch pianist?"

Why are pianist' fingers like lightening?
They rarely strike the same spot twice.

Chinese Proverb:
Foolish man give wife grand piano, wise man give wife upright organ.

Why did they invent keyboards? So musicians would have some place to put their beers.

How is Colonel Sanders like a typical keyboard player?
All he's concerned with is legs, breasts, and thighs.

Bass

Ten Signs You Need Music Lessons on Bass:
    10. You only play the roots of chords.
    9. The drummer has to help you compose a bass line.
    8. You think of Time as a magazine.
    7. Girls are *not* attracted to your bass lines!
    6. "I want to know how to get rich playing music."
    5. "I think I play better than Jaco."
    4. "I want to be a Star."

3. You spend more than 5 minutes with your tuner.

2. Asking everyone, "What's a diminish chord?"

And the biggest sign you need music lessons is...(ta-dum!)

1. "I studied note-scales and can play every scale in the book!!"

And, a special bonus indicator: "Of course I can play. I watch YouTube!"

She asked me to tell her the three words every girl wants to hear. So, I whispered, "I play bass" into her ear.

"Hey! Why don't you play a five-string bass? Is a five-string bass too hard for you...?"

"No, you idiot! Jaco didn't need five strings..."

"Dude, I think I figured out why all your solos sound so bad. That thing's actually a bass."

Groupie Accidentally Sleeps With Bass Player

LOUISVILLE, KY—The day after The Academy concert, Victoria Jorgensen, 22, was terrified to realize that she had accidentally slept with the band's bass player, mistaking him for someone important in the band.

"I can't believe how stupid I was," said Jorgensen. "I mean, I went up to the guy and was like, 'Are you in the band?' and he was all like, 'Yeah, I'm in the band,' so I did him. Then, this morning, I was telling my friends and I realized he was just the bass player. This happens to me all the time."

Jorgensen plans to do more research before sleeping with another band member. "This won't happen again," said Jorgensen. "If I'm going to sleep with someone, they'd better be important. I mean, I could find someone here in town as important as a bass player."

Adam Siska, The Academy's bass player, was unavailable for comment.

The Ten Commandments Of Bass

1. "Thou shalt not fuck up the groove. Fuck up the notes if thou must, but not the groove."
2. "Thou shalt not lust after thy guitar player's part. He keepeth the fun, thou keepeth the groove."
3. "Be thou not swayed by a drummer with crappy time, for thou art the keeper of the beat."
4. "Be thou not led into temptation before the gig. After is cool."
5. "Thou pusheth thy luck with five strings, six is a mortal sin, for thou hast no business in the upper register."
6. "Thou shalt not thump with thy thumb, nor honk with a pick when thy fingers are the way of truth."
7. "Thou shalt not fear whole notes, for they can be the way and the light."
8. "Thou shalt leave the fancy shit to thy bandmates, so they might wrestle with their own bad taste."
9. "Thou shalt change thy strings at least once per decade, whether they need it or not."
10. "Thou shalt tune thy bass before each and every gig, even though it was in tune when last thou put it away."

Dating a Musician?
(Why the Bass Player Will Pluck Your Strings)

If there were a Pocket Field Guide to Dating Musicians, it would read like this:

This species can best be viewed in its natural habitat, under the colored lights of nightclub stages — and in the drier months, anywhere there's free beer.

At the front stands the lead singer, scientific name *Egos maximus*, a close relative of the peacock. Don't look him directly in the eye; he views this as a mating call and will rip his ironic T-shirt right off and begin caressing the mike suggestively if he thinks you're the slightest bit interested.

To his left is the guitarist, *Controli freakata*, recognized in the wild by his rock-and-roll power stance, practiced indifference, and telltale markings: pants several sizes too small and bits of twine, locks of hair, and other strands of refuse wound round his wrist as boho jewelry. Beware: He is prone to depression; it's when he writes "his best stuff."

And making all that racket at the back, on the riser, is the grinning drummer, *Rhythm perspiratious*, descended more recently than the rest of us from apes. This good-time boy is a competent multitasker but frequently shamed by his bandmates for not knowing scales. Feeding habits: Large meat sandwiches that he stores in the bass drum and gnaws on between songs.

Then there's the keyboard player, who … Wait, no. This isn't 1985. There is no keyboard player.

But hark. What is that intriguing breed on the right? The one standing in the shadows with the quiet intensity and the booming, low-slung bass? That, my boyfriend-shopping adventurers, is the extraordinary *Fella perfectata* from the family *Delicieux*. His coat is less showy than the others', so he often goes unnoticed. Yet he's always there when you need him, steadily, deftly weaving the band's rhythm and melody into an impenetrable humming-thumping-humming-thumping musical fabric that— scientifically speaking—you just want to wrap yourself up in. Naked.

Listen, I've dated a lot of musicians. And if you're looking for a band member who can make your soul wail a power ballad, there's no better choice than a bass player. (This commentary is about men because that's how I roll, but Kim Gordon, Sheryl Crow, Aimee Mann, Suzi Quatro, Kim Deal, Rhonda Smith, Meshell Ndegeocello: respect.)

Here's why the bass player is the best rocker to pluck your strings:

- What's sexier than a man who doesn't need to be the center of attention — who's content to sit back and hold a thing together from the bottom up? That sort of hang-backedness speaks to a deep-rooted confidence, an honorable work ethic even, that can only be described as hotness amplified.

- There's something to be said about an instrument that makes your whole howdy-do rumble. And that something is this: "Yes, please."
- Bass players are classy. Think McCartney and Sting—not Flea, who's a drummer in bass players' clothing (which apparently is a tube sock). The very fact that you don't know who played bass for most of the great American bands is testament to the bass player's humility. And if modesty doesn't sound sexy, then wake up just once next to a lead singer — go on, I dare you — and see how quickly "unassuming" becomes music to your ears.
- Bass players don't care if you notice this, but theirs is the manliest instrument in a rock band. It's the biggest and heaviest. And the strings are rope-thick, which gives bass players strong fingers, and we'll just leave that right there.

To be clear, no one is suggesting you date a musician. They keep odd hours, are hard of hearing, and believe that actual income-generating work plays havoc with their carefully cultivated mellow.

Plus, you'll be expected to do a lot of stage-side swaying and swooning as though you hadn't heard that exact song played that exact way 17 kajillion times before.

But if your inner groupie simply won't be stifled, don't fret. Just snag yourself a four-stringed fella. And keep some earplugs handy.

—Starshine Roshell (Santa Barbara Independent)

What do you call 20 bass players skydiving from an airplane?
Skeet.

Why are bass players steering wheels so small?
So they can drive with handcuffs on.

Why don't bass players play hide and seek?
Because no one will look for them.

What are the three most difficult years in a bass player's life?
Second grade.

A man gives his son an electric bass for his 15th birthday, along with a coupon for four bass lessons. When the son returns from his first lesson, the father asks, "So, what did you learn?"

"Well, I learned the first five notes on the E string." Next week, after the second lesson, the father again asks about the progress, and the son replies, "This time I learned the first five notes on the A string."

One week later, the son comes home far later than expected, smelling of cigarettes and beer. "So," the father asks: "What happened in today's lesson?"

"Dad, I'm sorry I couldn't make it to my lesson; I had a gig!"

Did you hear about the bass player that was so bad even the lead singer noticed?

A tour manager comes across the guitarist and bass player fighting at the side of the stage and pulls them apart asking what the problem was. "That bastard detuned one of the strings on my bass", says the bass player, "And we're on stage in five minutes." "So, what's the problem?" asks the tour manager. "He won't tell me which string he detuned," said the bassist.

Late one day, six guys walked in to a local pub, obviously in pairs of two, sit down and order their favorite after-work drinks. The first two to seat themselves and be served by the bartender were two guys working at a major university whose I.Q.s were so high they could hardly be measured! They began discussing everything from Quantum Mechanics to the fine points of Particle Physics, each one as brilliantly as the other. The bartender then went over to the next pair who were "regular guys" with ordinary jobs and average IQs, schmoozing about how hard it was today to keep up with bill payments, how high taxes were, how corrupt politicians were and all the day-to-day struggles most everyone has. The last two the bartender served were two very badly educated, ill-mannered dolts with very low IQs that could barely be measured on any IQ test. As soon as they'd ordered, the bartender overheard one say to the other, "Oh, hey, I meant to ask ya, d'you use flat-wound or round-wound on your bass?"

Quite a number of years ago, the Seattle Symphony was doing Beethoven's *Symphony No. 9* under the baton of Milton Katims.
Now at this point, you must understand two things:
1. There's a quite long segment in this symphony where the basses don't have a thing to do. Not a single note for page after page.
2. There used to be a tavern called *Dez's 400*, right across the street from the Seattle Opera House, rather favored by local musicians.

It had been decided that during this performance, once the bass players had played their parts in the opening of the symphony, they were to quietly lay down their instruments and leave the stage, rather than sit on their stools looking and feeling dumb for twenty minutes. Once they got backstage, someone suggested that they trot across the street and quaff a few brews.

When they got there, a European nobleman recognized that they were musicians, and bought them several rounds of drinks. Two of the bassists passed out, and the rest of the section, not to mention the nobleman, were rather drunk. Finally, one of them looked at his watch and exclaimed, "Look at the time! We'll be late!"

The remaining bassists tried in vain to wake up their section mates, but finally those who were still conscious had to give up and run across the street to the Opera House.

While they were on their way in, the bassist who suggested this excursion in the first place said, "I think we'll still have enough time--I anticipated that something like this could happen, so I tied a string around the last pages of the score. When he gets down to there, Milton's going to have to slow the tempo way down while he waves the baton with one hand and fumbles with the string with the other."

Sure enough, when they got back to the stage they hadn't missed their entrance, but one look at their conductor's face told them they were still in serious trouble. Katims was furious! After all,

It was the bottom of the *Ninth*, the basses were loaded, the score was tied, there were two men out, and the Count was full.

How do you tell if a bassist is actually dead?
Hold out a check (but don't be fooled: a slight, residual, spasmodic clutching action may occur even hours after the death occurred).

After years of hiding the fact that their love is gone, and after their last child moves out, Mom and Dad announce they're getting a divorce. The kids are distraught and hire a marriage counselor as a last resort in the hopes of keeping their parents together. The counselor works for hours, tries all of his methods, but the couple still won't talk to each other. Finally, he goes over to a closet, brings out a beautiful upright bass and begins to play.

After a minute or so, the couple starts talking and they discover that they're not actually that far apart and decide to give their marriage another try. The kids are amazed and ask the counselor how he managed to do it. He replies, "I've never seen a couple who wouldn't talk through a bass solo."

How do you get two bass players to play in unison?
Hand them charts a half-step apart.

What do you do if you run over a bass player?
Back up.

What do you throw a drowning bass player?
His amp.

Drums

We'll Get The Best Snare Sound Ever!

The Nerve...!

My next-door neighbor had the audacity to knock on my door last night at 3AM. Can you believe it? 3 AM! Lucky for him, I was still up playing my drums!

"Listen to the reverb on that snare!"
Said NO ONE, EVER.

"Dude! Chill! I was joking. Your dad's not a drummer. Ok?"

Friends don't let friends clap on one and three.

Said the guitar player to the turtle, the band's new drummer:
"Either play faster or get out of the band."

A scientist was studying native culture in the darkest reaches of Africa. All of a sudden, drums start playing. After what seemed like an eternity, the scientist had had enough and complained bitterly to the Chief of the tribe he was studying. "Why are the drums playing so long? Surely, enough is enough," he said. The chief was patient with the scientist, explaining, "Drums play - good omen, drums stop playing - bad omen." Unfortunately for the scientist, the drums went on - hour after hour, day after day. The scientist would rant and rave to the chief and each time the chief would say, "Drums play - good omen, drums stop playing bad omen." Suddenly, and without warning, the drums stopped. This completely unnerved the scientist who ran up to the chief fearing the worst. "The drums stopped, the drums stopped! What's going to happen? What's going to happen?" he screamed, tearing his hair out. The chief looked at him calmly and replied, "Bass solo."

What's the last thing a drummer says before getting kicked out of the band?
1. "Hey, I've got some songs too!"
2. "Can't we split the publishing equally?"

What's the difference between a drummer and a toilet?
A toilet only has to deal with one asshole at a time.

What has three legs and a prick?
A drum stool.

Lennon was once asked if Ringo was the best drummer in the world, he replied, "He's not even the best drummer in The Beatles!"

What do you call someone who hangs around with musicians?
A drummer.

What did the drummer get on his IQ test?
Drool.

What does it mean when the drummer drools equally out of both sides of his mouth?
The stage is level.

Why do drummers have a half-ounce more brains than horses?
So they don't disgrace themselves in the parade.

What is the similarity between a drum solo and a sneeze?
You can tell it's coming but you can't do anything about it!

Why are orchestra intermissions limited to 20 minutes?
So you don't have to retrain the drummers.

How do you get a drummer to play an accelerando?
Ask him to play in 4/4 at a steady 120 bpm.

How do you know when a drummer is knocking at your door?
The knock always slows down.

"Hey buddy, how late does the band play?"
"Oh, about a half beat behind the drummer."

Why are drummers always tapping their fingers?
They're rehearsing.

What does it mean when a drummer is in your bed gasping for air and calling your name?
You didn't hold the pillow down long enough.

Why do drummers date smart women?
Opposites attract.

How can you tell when a drummer is well hung?
When you can just barely slip your finger in between his neck and the noose.

How do you get a drummer to stop biting his nails?
Make him wear shoes.

What's the best way to make a drummer do sit-ups?
Put the remote control between his toes.

What's the difference between Big Foot and an intelligent drummer?
Big Foot has been spotted several times.

Why do bands have bass players?
To translate for the drummer.

Did you hear about the time the bass player locked his keys in his car?
It took two hours to get the drummer out.

What's the difference between a drummer and a drum machine?
With a drum machine, you only have to punch the information in once.

Heard backstage: "Will the musicians and the drummer please come to the stage!"

A drummer in a big band is having trouble with his time. He keeps getting behind the beat and the band is getting fed up and they go to the leader and ask that he be fired. However, the leader says he's known the guy forever, he's always been a good drummer, and he'll talk to the guy and see what the problem is. He goes to the drummer who admits he's having problems and says he's working on it and to please not fire him. But things just get worse. He keeps slowing down the beat and coming in late and finally the whole band threatens to quit. The leader has to fire him. The drummer is so depressed that he goes down to the railroad tracks and throws himself behind a train.

What's the similarity between a drummer and a philosopher?
They both perceive time as an abstract concept.

What do you say to a drummer in a three-piece suit?
Will the defendant please rise?

One night, the front man said to the drummer, "When the band starts to swing, I want you to play more on the ride cymbal." The drummer replied, "When the band starts to swing will you please raise your hand?"

A drummer is being ridiculed by his band, "You're not a real musician. You don't know anything about music." Depressed, he decides to prove he is indeed a "real musician" by taking up another instrument to show that he knows something about music. He goes to a pawnshop to buy a secondhand instrument. He says to the owner, "I'm a drummer and I'm tired of being put down as a non-musician. I want to learn another instrument to show that I really do know about music. I've looked over your stuff and I've decided to take either the red trumpet or the accordion. How much are they?" The pawnshop owner says, "Well, the fire extinguisher I can let you have pretty cheap, but the radiator has to stay here."

How do you get a drummer off your porch?
Pay for the pizza.

What does every band need?
Three musicians and a drummer.

A group of cowboys were waiting in their fort for the Indians to attack. They listened to the distant pounding war drums. One cowboy muttered to another, "I don't like the sound of them drums." Just then, a distant voice came over the hill, "He's not our regular drummer!"

One day, a tuba player wanted to torture the drummer behind him, so he hid one of the drummer's sticks. After looking around for a few minutes, with a frantic, wide-eyed expression, the drummer fell to his knees, flung his arms wide, and screamed to heaven: "Finally! A miracle, after all these years! I'm a Conductor!"

The Greatest Drummer In The World

In the summer of 1969, a mail sorter at a New York post office received a letter addressed "To the Greatest Drummer in the World." There was no address or return address and the sorter wasn't sure what to do.

Fortunately, there was a former drummer who worked the front counter of the Post Office who promptly found Max Roach's address and forwarded the letter. Max Roach received the letter and said, "Oh no, I'm not the greatest drummer in the world." Max then promptly forwarded the letter to Gene Krupa, who said, "Somebody must've made a mistake." Gene then forwarded the letter on to Buddy Rich (known for his incredible ego and abuse of his band members for every little mistake they made).

Of course, Buddy had been waiting his entire life for that moment. He read the words "To the Greatest Drummer in the World" and smiled from ear-to-ear as he ripped open the envelope.

He began to read the letter, "Dear Ringo...."

In New York City, an out of work jazz drummer named Ed was thinking of throwing himself off a bridge. But then, he ran into a former booking agent who told him about the fantastic opportunities for drummers in Iraq. The agent said, "If you can find your way over there, just take my card and look up the bandleader named Faisal--he's the large guy with the beard wearing gold pajamas and shoes that curl up at the toes."

Ed hit up everyone he knew and borrowed enough to buy transport to Iraq. It took several days to arrange for passport, visas, transportation into Iraq and the shipping of his equipment, but he was finally on his way. Ed arrived in Baghdad and immediately started searching for Faisal. He found guys in pajamas of every color but gold.

Finally, in a small coffeehouse, he saw a huge man with a beard--wearing gold pajamas and shoes that curled up at the toes! Ed approached him and asked if he was Faisal. He was. Ed gave him the agent's card and Faisal's face brightened into a huge smile. "You're just in time--I need you for a gig tonight. Meet me at the market near the mosque at 7:30 with your equipment." "But," gasped Ed, "What about a rehearsal?" "No time--don't worry." And with that, Faisal disappeared.

Ed arrived in the market at 7:00 to set up his gear. He introduced himself to the other musicians, who were all playing instruments he had never seen in his life. At 7:30 sharp, Faisal appeared and hopped on the bandstand, his gold pajamas glittering in the twilight. Without a word to the musicians, he lifted his arm for the downbeat. "Wait." shouted Ed. "What are we playing?" Faisal shot him a look of frustration and shouted back, "Fake it! Just give me heavy after-beats on 7 and 13."

Two drummers and a violinist decide to form a band. The three of them start playing, and the sound is just awful. One drummer turns to the other and says, "We sound terrible. I don't think this is going to work. Let's get rid of the violinist."

Guitar

Uh Oh...

"Who needs rhythm? I play LEAD!

Picasso's Blues Period

Sung with lament, accompanied by acoustic guitar:

"Got a woman with both eyes on one side of her face—and her nose is upside down."

"Said I got a woman with both eyes on one side of her face—and her nose is upside down."

Social Media Explained to Guitarists

Twitter: I'm playing my #guitar.

Facebook: I like to play my guitar.

Foursquare: This is where I play my guitar.

Instagram: Here's a vintage photograph of my guitar.

YouTube: Here I am, playing my guitar.

LinkedIn: My skills include playing guitar.

Pinterest: Here's a picture of my favorite guitar.

Last FM: Now listening to "Guitar Playing."

G+: I'm a Google employee who plays guitar.

Marketing Explained to Guitarists

1—You see a gorgeous girl at a party, you go up to her and say, "I am a great guitarist. Marry me."

That's called Direct Marketing.

2—You attend a party and your friend goes up to a girl and points at you, telling her, "He's a great guitarist. Marry him."

That's called Advertising.

3—A girl walks up to you and says, "You are a great guitarist. Will you marry me?"

That's called Brand Recognition.

4—You say to another girl, "I'm a great guitarist. Marry me." She hauls off and slaps you silly.

That's called Customer Feedback.

5—Before you can say, "I'm a great guitarist. Marry me," to one more girl, your wife arrives at the party.

That's called Restriction from Entering a New Market.

What is the difference between a rocker and a jazzman?
A rocker plays 3 chords in front of 3,000 people.
A jazzman plays 3,000 chords in front of 3 people.

Christmas Dreams Do Come True
Older Brother: "Oh boy! A new air guitar!!!"
Younger Brother: "Can I have your old one?"

No Problem Here

Don't worry. We'll just stand in complete silence while you figure out which pedal is making the weird hum. It's not like we're paying for rehearsal time, or anything…

It Works

My girlfriend left a note on my Marshall amp. "It's not working. I can't take anymore. I am leaving."

I switched on the amp, flicked the standby on, volume up and hit a chord…PERFECT!

What the hell is she talking about?

The Perfect Roadies—They Work Like Dogs!
(Courtesy of James Saez)

Musician with his guitar case approaches the customs officer at the airport. "Sir, you can't take that any further," said the officer, pointing at the guitar case. "New regulations?" asked the musician. "No," the officer replied, "I heard your last album."

My biggest fear is when I die, my wife will sell my guitars for what I told her they cost.

Word!

There's nowhere I'd rather be than here, with my guitar, reviewing the Phrygian mode and boning up on my half-diminished 7th chords.

Being a good guitar player is 3% talent and 97% not being distracted by the Internet.

You Might Be a Guitarist If…
1. The gear in your trunk is worth more than your car.
2. You think a G-String is something made of phosphor bronze.
3. You have a photo of your guitar on your phone.
4. You play another guitar and feel guilty for cheating.
5. You have at least five picks in your possession at all times.
6. Your pet names are "Slash," "Hendrix," and "Page."
7. You've never had to remove furniture to make room for an amp.

For those who don't know

These are **sharps**,
not #hashtags.

Guide to Criticizing Guitarists

Who	Just Say
Awesome shredder	That guy has chops but his playing has no soul.
Soul guitarist	That guy has no chops.
Classical guitarist	Geeze. That'll never get you laid.
Any blues player who respects and draws inspiration from Stevie Ray Vaughan	What a rip off. He's just a Stevie wannabe.
Stevie Ray Vaughan	What a rip-off. He was just a Freddie King wannabe.
John Mayer	What a douche.
Guitarist in any band that actually sells CDs and gets stuff on the radio these days	What a sell out. Or, nobody listens to that crap.
Anyone awesome enough to get even remotely close to achieving Eric Johnson-esque tone	What a Rip-off. Another Eric Johnson clone.

Eric Clapton	I don't get what the fuss is about. He's just another white British guy who wishes he were an American black guy.
Singer/songwriter who plays but can't burn	That girl sucks.
Guitarist with a real job who can afford an incredible rig	Somebody go tell that guy that money can't buy him tone.
MIDI guitar player	Cheater.
Guitarist with a digital modeling guitar or amp	Too bad his tone sucks.
Guitarist with a solid state amp	Too bad his tone sucks.
Any guitarist on YouTube	That guy's tone sucks.

Guitarist in a punk band	That guy can't even play.
Any bar band guitarist playing covers	How unoriginal. Gimme a break.
Any bar band guitarist playing originals	How self-indulgent. Gimme a break.
Guitarist with several big-brand endorsements	What an endorsement whore.
Guitarist with several small-brand endorsements	What a douche.
Electric player who uses .009 gauge strings or lower	What a wuss.
Electric player who uses .011 gauge strings or higher	Yeah, right.
Guy guitarist you've never heard of before	He's okay. Not my thing, but I can see how some people like him.
Girl guitarist you've never heard of before	She sucks.

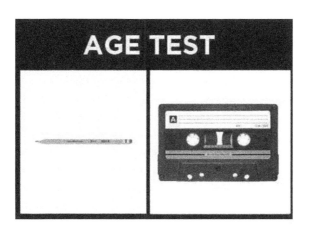

It was the first day of school and the teacher thought she'd get to know the kids by asking them their names and what their fathers did for a living. The first little girl said, "My name is Mary and my daddy is a postman." The next little boy said, "I'm Andy and my dad is a mechanic." It was little Johnny's turn and he said, "My name is Johnny and my father is a striptease dancer in a cabaret for gay men." The teacher gasped and quickly moved on, but later, in the school yard, the teacher approached Johnny privately and asked if it's really true that his dad dances nude in a gay bar. Little Johnny blushed and said, "No, he's really a guitar player in a country band, but I was too embarrassed to say so."

Female guitarist shouting at her husband in a crowded shopping center: "Don't forget, honey, I need a new 'G' string!"

How do you get a guitar player to turn down?
Put a chart in front of him.

How do you get a guitar player to stop playing?
Put notes on the chart.

The producer asked the guitar player to play with more dynamics...to which the guitarist replied, "Dynamics? I'm playing as loud as I can!"

What do you call a guitar player that only knows two chords?
A music critic.

If you threw a guitarist and a harmonica player off a cliff, which one would hit the ground first?
The guitarist. The harmonica player would have to stop half way down to ask what key they were in.

What are the two most frequent guitarist lies?
1. I'm not too loud
2. I already turned down

An old man was sitting in the park, playing his guitar when a little boy walked up and stood watching him. This was a little bitty feller, stood about three feet high. When the old man finished his song, the little feller spoke up and said, "I play guitar too." The man said, "How long have you been playing?" The youngster told him, "About a year." Then the old man said, "Well, do you play like I do?" and the little boy said, "No, but I used to."

A guitar player says to his wife, "Oh baby, I can play you just like my guitar." His wife replies, "I'd rather have you play me like your harmonica!"

What's the difference between a jazz guitarist and a large pizza?
A large pizza can feed a family of four.

Did you hear about the guitarist who was in tune?
Neither did I.

How many guitarists does it take to cover a Stevie Ray Vaughan tune?
Evidently all of them.

Two guys were walking down the street. One was destitute… the other was a guitar player as well.

What's the difference between a guitarist and a bag of garbage?
The garbage gets taken out at least once a week.

Why do guitarists make great astronauts?
Because they all take up space in school.

Why are scientists breeding guitarists instead of rats for science experiments?
Because they breed faster and you don't get as attached to them.

Why did the post office recall all the new guitar player stamps?
Because people couldn't tell which side to spit on.

If you see a guitar player on a bicycle why should you swerve to avoid hitting him?
Because it might be your bicycle.

You're trapped in a room with a tiger, a rattlesnake, and a guitar player. You have a gun with two bullets. What should you do?
Shoot the guitarist. Twice.

Why do only 10% of guitarists make it to Heaven?
Because if they all went, it would be Hell.

How does a guitar player show he's planning for the future?
He buy's two cases of beer instead of one.

What's a guitar player's idea of honesty?
Telling you his real name.

What do you call two guitarists playing in unison?
Counterpoint.

What do a vacuum cleaner and an electric guitar have in common?
Both suck when you plug them in.

What did the guitarist do when his teacher told him to turn his amplifier on?
He caressed it softly and told it that he loved it.

What's the best thing to play on a guitar?
Solitaire.

What do a cup of coffee and Eric Clapton have in common?
They both suck without Cream.

A guitar player comes to the doctor and complains about a serious deterioration of his memory. He especially has a hard time remembering correct changes and is afraid to lose all his gigs. Since the doctor can't find the cause, he asks the guitarist to leave behind his brain for a week in his lab for more detailed examinations. After seven days, the guitar player fails to show up, and even after two more weeks, there's no sign of him. Finally, the doctor runs into him on the street, grabs him and asks: "Excuse me, but your brain is still waiting for you to stop by and pick it up, so why don't you show up?" The guitarist says, "Well, I think you can keep it; I finally switched to bass..."

Guitarist writes to the "Dear Abby" help column:

Dear Abby,

I think my wife is cheating on me.

I am a working musician and, as you would expect, I travel a lot.

I have been noticing strange things happening when I get home. Her mobile phone rings and she steps outside to answer it or she says, "I'll call you back later." When I ask her who called she gets evasive.

Sometimes she goes out with friends and comes home late, getting dropped off around the corner and walking the rest of the way.

I once picked up the extension while she was on the phone and she got very angry.

A buddy of mine plays guitar in a band. He told me that my wife and some guy have been to his gigs.

He wanted to borrow my guitar amp. That's when I got the idea to find out for myself what was really happening. I said, "Sure, you can use my amp but I want to hide behind it at the gig and see if she comes into the venue and who she comes in with." He agreed.

Saturday night came and I slipped behind my Marshall JCM800 half stack to get a good view. I could feel the heat coming off the back of the amp. It was at that moment, crouching down behind the amp, that I noticed that one of the tubes was not glowing as bright as the other 3.

Is this something I can fix myself or do need to take it to a technician?

Thanks - Very Concerned.

The guitarist finishes his gig and is the last one in the place with the barman, who asks if he'd like a scotch before he goes home. The player says, "Sure," and the barman plonks down a big glass of the juice and a little bowl of peanuts to go with it, and then wanders off to wipe down the counter. This leaves the guitarist all by himself for a minute. From nowhere a little voice says, "Great gig man, you're one hot picker."

The player looks at the barman and says, "Thanks," and the barman says, "What for?" and the player says, "For sayin' nice things about my work." The barman says, "I didn't say nothing."

The guitarist thinks it's late and he's a bit spaced, so he'd better head off when another little voice says, "Yeah, great licks man and nice moves too, you sure can cut it up there." The guitar player turns around and says, "Thanks," but there's nobody there. The feller at the bar says, "Are you ok?" cause the picker looks a bit pale and the guitarist says, "Yeah, I think so."

Then, as he empties his glass, another voice says, "Hot licks, great look, wonderful style man, the chicks sure got off on you!" and the bloke says, "OK! THAT'S IT! WHAT'S GOING ON HERE?"

The barman runs down and says, "What's your problem dude?" to which the guitarist says, "WHERE ARE THOSE VOICES COMING FROM? IS THIS CANDID CAMERA?"

"What voices? What are they saying?"

When the guitarist tells the barman what was going on and what was said, the barman says, "Oh, that'll be the peanuts man, they're complementary!"

Why Guitars Are Better Than Women
- A guitar has a volume knob.
- If you break a guitar's G-string, it only costs $.79 for a new one.
- You can unplug a guitar.
- If your guitar doesn't make sounds you like, you can retune it.
- If your guitar strings are too heavy, you can just get a lighter set.
- You can have a guitar professionally adjusted to your liking.
- You can go to a guitar shop and play all the guitars you want for free.
- You can take lessons on how to play a guitar without feeling embarrassed.
- You can rent a guitar without worrying about who rented it before you.
- You can get rich playing a guitar, not broke.
- A guitar doesn't take half of everything you own when you sell it.
- You can share your Guitar with your friends.
- Guitars don't care how many other Guitars you've played.
- Guitars don't care if you look at other Guitars.
- Guitars don't care if you buy Guitar magazines.
- Your Guitar doesn't care if you never listen to it.
- Your Guitar won't care if you leave the toilet seat up.
- Your parents won't remain in touch with your old Guitar after you dump it.
- Guitars don't insult you if you're a bad player.
- Your Guitar never wants a night out with the other Guitars.
- You can play your Guitar the first time you meet it, without having to take it to dinner, see a movie, or meet its mother.

Why Guitars Are Better Than Men

- Guitars don't snore.
- Guitars never wake you up in the middle of the night, for any reason.
- Guitars never try to show you off to their friends.
- Guitars don't come home drunk after a night out with the other Guitars.
- You don't have to praise a Guitar after playing it.
- Guitars don't have to prove anything and they don't have egos.
- Guitars don't try to change you once you've bought them.
- Second-hand Guitars don't go to see previous owners when you're out of town.
- You don't have to continually assure your Guitar that its string length is just right.
- Your Guitar will never earn more than you do for the same job just because it's a Guitar.
- Your Guitar never spends a night out with other Guitars and comes home with a strange rash on its fret board.

conDuctor

A musician calls the symphony office to talk to the conductor. "I'm sorry, he's dead," comes the reply. The musician calls back 25 times, always getting the same reply from the receptionist. At last she asks him why he keeps calling. "I just like to hear you say it."

What's the difference between a bull and an orchestra?
On a bull the horns are in the front and the asshole is in the back.

If an all-brass band is playing on an open field and a thunderstorm starts, who is most likely to be hit by lightning?
The conductor.

Why are conductor's hearts so coveted for transplants?
They've had so little use.

What's the difference between a conductor and a sack of shit?
Just the sack.

If you drop a conductor and a watermelon off a tall building, which will hit the ground first?
Who cares?

A conductor and a violist are standing in the middle of the road. Which one do you run over first, and why?
The conductor. Business before pleasure.

What do you have when a group of conductors are up to their necks in wet concrete?
Not enough concrete.

Did you hear about the planeload of conductors en route to the European Festival?
The good news: it crashed.
The bad news: there were three empty seats on board.

What's the difference between a pig and a symphony orchestra conductor?
There are some things a pig just isn't willing to do.

What is the ideal weight for a conductor?
About 2 1/2 lbs., including the urn.

Why is a conductor like a condom?
It's safer with one, but more fun without.

What's the definition of an assistant conductor?
A mouse trying to become a rat.

What's the difference between alto clef and Greek?
Some conductors actually read Greek.

What do you do with a horn player that can't play?
Give him two sticks, put him in the back, and call him a percussionist.

What do you do if he can't do that?
Take away one of the sticks, put him up front, and call him a conductor.

A new conductor was at his first rehearsal. It was not going well. He was as wary of the musicians as they were of him. As he left the rehearsal room, the timpanist sounded a rude little "bong." The angry conductor turned and said, "All right! Who did that?"

Four cowboys are sitting on a mountain one night having a few cold ones around a campfire, one a tuba player, one a trumpet player, one a conductor and the other a trombone player. The tuba player tosses an empty can of Budweiser into the air, whips out his gun, and shoots it declaring, "I just killed the king of beers!" The trumpet player, not wanting to be outdone, tosses his empty can of Coors into the air, shoots it and declares "Ha! I just shot the silver bullet!" The trombone player, ever so suave, reaches into his pack, pulls out a bottle of Michelob, calmly drinks the whole thing, tosses his bottle into the air and shoots the conductor. Grinning broadly at his fellow players, he says, "Guys, it just doesn't get any better than this."

What's the difference between a conductor and a stagecoach driver?
The stagecoach driver only has to look at four horses' asses.

It was the night of the big symphony concert, and all the town notables showed up to hear it. However, it was getting close to 8 o'clock and the conductor hadn't yet shown up. The theater's manager was getting desperate, knowing that he'd have to refund everyone's money if he cancelled the concert, so he went backstage and asked all the musicians if any could conduct.
None of them could, so he went around and asked the staff if any of them could conduct. He had no luck there either, so he started asking people in the lobby, in the hope that maybe one of them could conduct the night's concert.

He still hadn't found anyone, so he went outside and started asking everybody passing by if they could conduct. He had no luck whatsoever and by this time the concert was 15 minutes late in starting. The assistant manager came out to say that the crowd was getting restless and about ready to demand their money back.

The desperate manager looked around and spied a cat, a dog, and a horse standing in the street. "Oh, what the heck," he exclaimed, "Let's ask them--what do we have to lose?"

So, the manager and assistant manager went up to the cat, and the manager asked, "Mr. cat, do you know how to conduct?" The cat meowed "I don't know, I'll try," but though it tried really hard, it just couldn't stand upright on its hind legs. The manager sighed and thanked the cat, and then moved on to the dog.

"Mr. dog," he asked, "Do you think you can conduct?" The dog woofed, "Let me see," but although it was able to stand up on its hind legs and wave its front paws around, it just couldn't keep upright long enough to last through an entire movement.

"Well, nice try," the manager told the dog, and with a sigh of resignation turned to the horse. "Mr. horse," he asked, "How about you--can you conduct?" The horse looked at him for a second and then without a word turned around, presented its hind end, and started swishing its tail in perfect four-four time.

"That's it!" the manager exclaimed, "The concert can go on!" However, right then the horse dropped a load of plop onto the street. The assistant manager was horrified, and he told the manager "We can't have this horse conduct! What would the orchestra think?"

The manager looked first at the horse's rear end and then at the plop lying in the street and replied, "Trust me--from this angle, the orchestra won't even know they have a new conductor!"

Once upon a time, there was a blind rabbit and blind snake, both living in the same neighborhood. One beautiful day, the blind rabbit was hopping happily down the path toward his home, when he bumped into someone. Apologizing profusely, he explained, "I am blind, and didn't see you there."

"Perfectly all right," said the snake, "Because I am blind, too, and did not see to step out of your way."

A conversation followed, gradually becoming more intimate, and finally the snake said, "This is the best conversation I have had with anyone for a long time. Would you mind if I felt you to see what you are like?"

"Why, no," said the rabbit. "Go right ahead."

So, the snake wrapped himself around the rabbit and shuffled and snuggled his coils, and said, "MMMM! You're soft and warm and fuzzy and cuddly...and those ears! You must be a rabbit."

"Why, that's right!" said the rabbit. "May I feel you?"

"Go right ahead." said the snake, stretching himself out full length on the path.

The rabbit began to stroke the snake's body with his paws, and then drew back in disgust. "Yuck!" he said. "You're cold...and slimy... you must be a conductor!"

A guy walks into a pet store wanting a parrot. The store clerk shows him two beautiful ones out on the floor. "This one's $5,000 and the other is $10,000." the clerk said.

"Wow! What does the $5,000 one do?"

"This parrot can sing every aria Mozart ever wrote."

"And the other?" said the customer.

"This one can sing Wagner's entire Ring cycle. There's another one in the back room for $30,000."

"Holy moly! What does that one do?"

"Nothing that I can tell, but the other two parrots call him 'Maestro.'"

A violinist was auditioning for the Halle orchestra in England. After his audition, he was talking with the conductor. "What do you think about Brahms?" asked the conductor. "Ah..." the violinist replied, "Brahms is a great guy! Real talented musician. In fact, he and I were just playing some duets together last week!"

The conductor was impressed. "And what do you think of Mozart?" he asked him. "Oh, he's just swell! I just had dinner with him last week!" replied the violinist. Then the violinist looked at his watch and said he had to leave to catch the 1:30 train to London.

Afterwards, the conductor was discussing him with the board members. He said he felt very uneasy about hiring this violinist, because there seemed to be a serious credibility gap. The conductor knew for certain that there was no 1:30 train to London.

The following program notes are from an unidentified piano recital.

Tonight's page turner, Ruth Spelke, studied under Ivan Schmertnick at the Boris Nitsky School of Page Turning in Philadelphia. She has been turning pages here and abroad for many years for some of the world's leading pianists.

In 1988, Ms. Spelke won the Wilson Page Turning Scholarship, which sent her to Israel to study page turning from left to right. She is winner of the 1984 Rimsky Korsakov *Flight of the Bumblebee Prestissimo Medal*, having turned 47 pages in an unprecedented 32 seconds.

She was also a 1983 silver medalist at the Klutz Musical Page Pickup Competition: contestants retrieve and rearrange a musical score dropped from a Yamaha. Ms. Spelke excelled in "grace, swiftness, and especially poise."

For techniques, Ms. Spelke performs both the finger licking and the bent-page corner methods. She works from a standard left bench position, and is the originator of the dipped-elbow page snatch, a style used to avoid obscuring the pianist's view of the music.

She is page-turner in residence in Fairfield Iowa, where she occupies the coveted Alfred Hitchcock Chair at the Fairfield Page Turning Institute.

Ms. Spelke is married, and has a nice house on a lake.

COWBELL (DON'T FEAR) THE REAPER

WORDS AND MUSIC BY DONALD "BUCK DHARMA" ROESER

AS RECORDED BY THE BAND BLUE OYSTER CULT

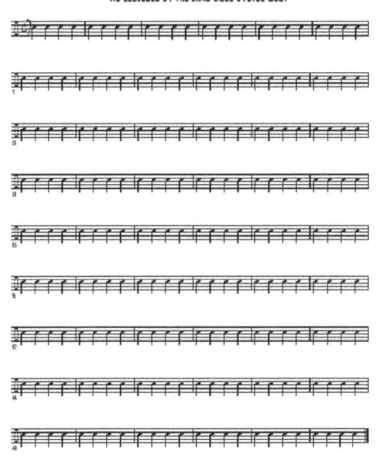

A Player's Guide for Keeping Conductors in Line

If there were a basic training manual for orchestra players, it might include ways to practice not only music, but one-upmanship. It seems as if many young players take pride in getting the conductor's goat.

The following rules are intended as a guide to the development of habits that will irritate the conductor. (Variations and additional methods depend upon the imagination and skill of the player.)

1. Never be satisfied with the tuning note. Fussing about the pitch takes attention away from the podium and puts it on you, where it belongs.
2. When raising the music stand, be sure the top comes off and spills the music on the floor.
3. Complain about the temperature of the rehearsal room, the lighting, crowded space, or a draft. It's best to do this when the conductor is under pressure.
4. Look the other way just before cues.
5. Never have the proper mute, a spare set of strings, or extra reeds. Percussion players must never have all their equipment.
6. Ask for a re-audition or seating change. Ask often. Give the impression you're about to quit. Let the conductor know you're there as a personal favor.
7. Pluck the strings as if you are checking tuning at every opportunity, especially when the conductor is giving instructions. Brass players: drop mutes. Percussionists have a wide variety of droppable items, but cymbals are unquestionably the best because they roll around for several seconds.
8. Loudly blow water from the keys during pauses (Horn, oboe and clarinet players are trained to do this from birth).
9. Long after a passage has gone by, ask the conductor if your C# was in tune. This is especially effective if you had no C# or were not playing at the time. (If he catches you, pretend to be correcting a note in your part.)
10. At dramatic moments in the music (while the conductor is emoting) be busy marking your music so that the climaxes will sound empty and disappointing.
11. Wait until well into a rehearsal before letting the conductor know you don't have the music.
12. Look at your watch frequently. Shake it in disbelief occasionally.
13. Tell the conductor, "I can't find the beat." Conductors are always sensitive about their "stick technique," so challenge it frequently.

14. Ask the conductor if he has listened to the Bernstein recording of the piece. Imply that he could learn a thing or two from it. It's also good ask, "Is this the first time you've conducted this piece?"
15. When rehearsing a difficult passage, screw up your face and shake your head indicating that you'll never be able to play it. Don't say anything: make him wonder.
16. If your articulation differs from that of others playing the same phrase, stick to your guns. Do not ask the conductor which is correct until backstage just before the concert.
17. Find an excuse to leave rehearsal about 15 minutes early so that others will become restless and start to pack up and fidget.
18. During applause, smile weakly or show no expression at all. Better yet, nonchalantly put away your instrument. Make the conductor feel he is keeping you from doing something really important. It is time that players reminded their conductors of the facts of life: just who do conductors think they are, anyway?

A conductor was having a lot of trouble with one drummer. He constantly gave this guy personal attention and much advice, but his performance simply didn't improve. Finally, before the whole orchestra, he said, "When a musician just can't handle his instrument and doesn't improve when given help, they take away the instrument, give him two sticks, and make him a drummer." A stage whisper was heard from the percussion section, "And if he can't handle even that, they take away one of his sticks and make him a conductor."

Violin

Why should you never try to drive a roof nail with a violin?
You might bend the roof nail.

Where does one find the obituaries of string players?
Under "Civic Improvements."

What's the difference between a violinist and a dog?
The dog knows when to stop scratching.

How do you make the violin sound like a viola?
Sit in the back and don't play.

How can you tell if a violin is out of tune?
The bow is moving.

A first violinist, a second violinist, a virtuoso violist, and a bass player are at the four corners of a football field. At the signal, someone drops a 100-dollar bill in the middle of the field and they run to grab it. Who gets it?

The second violinist, because:

No first violinist is going anywhere for only 100 dollars.

There's no such thing as a virtuoso violist.

The bass player hasn't figured out what it's all about.

Why did the Philharmonic disband?
Excessive sax and violins.

What's the difference between a violin and a viola?
There is no difference. The violin just looks smaller because the violinist's head is so much bigger.

What's the difference between a violin and a fiddle?
A fiddle is fun to listen to.

Why are viola jokes so short?
So violinists can understand them.

String players' motto: "It's better to be sharp than out of tune."

Why is a violinist like a SCUD missile?
Both are offensive and inaccurate.

Why don't viola players suffer from hemorrhoids?
Because all the assholes are in the first violin section.

What's the difference between a fiddle and a violin?
No one minds if you spill beer on a fiddle.

Why do violinists put a cloth between their chin and their instrument?
Violins don't have spit valves.

Jacques Thibault, the violinist, was once handed an autograph book by a fan while in the greenroom after a concert. "There's not much room on this page," he said. "What shall I write?" Another violinist, standing by, offered the following helpful hint: "Write your repertoire."

Little Harold was practicing the violin in the living room while his father was trying to read in the den. The family dog was lying in the den, and as the screeching sounds of little Harold's violin reached his ears, he began to howl loudly. The father listened to the dog and the violin as long as he could. Then he jumped up, slammed his paper to the floor and yelled above the noise, "For pity's sake, can't you play something the dog doesn't know?"

"Haven't I seen your face before?" a judge demanded, looking down at the defendant. "You have, Your Honor," the man answered hopefully. "I gave your son violin lessons last winter." "Ah, yes," recalled the judge. "Twenty years!"

How does a violinist's brain cell die?
Alone.

Three violin manufacturers have all done business for years on the same block in the small town of Cremona, Italy. After years of a peaceful co-existence, the Amati shop decided to put a sign in the window saying: "We make the best violins in Italy." The Guarneri shop soon followed suit, and put a sign in their window proclaiming: "We make the best violins in the world." Finally, the Stradivarius family put a sign out at their shop saying: "We make the best violins on the block."

Viola

A violinist was in a long line at the grocery store. As he got to the register he realized he had forgotten to get condoms. So, he asked the checkout girl if she would have some condoms brought up to the register. She asked, "What size condoms?" The violinist replied that he didn't know. She asked him to drop his pants. He did, she reached over the counter, grabbed hold of him, then picked up the store intercom and said, "One box of large condoms to register 5." The next man in line, who was a cellist, thought this was interesting, and like most of us, up for a cheap thrill. When he got to the register, he told the checker that he too had forgotten to get condoms, and asked if she could have some brought up to the register. She asked him what size, and he stated that he didn't know. She asked him to drop his pants. He did, she gave him a quick feel, picked up the intercom and said, "One box of medium condoms to register 5. "A few customers back was a violist. He thought what he had witnessed was way too cool. He had never had sexual contact with a live female, so he thought this was his chance. When he got up to the register, he told the checker he needed some condoms. She asked him what size, and he stated that he didn't know. She asked him to drop his pants. He did, she gave him one quick squeeze, picked up the intercom and said, "Clean up at register 5."

Did you hear about the violist who bragged he could play 32nd notes? The rest of the orchestra didn't believe him, so he proved it by playing one.

What's the difference between violists and terrorists?
Terrorists have sympathizers.

What do you do with a dead violist?
Move him to the back row.

How do you get a violist to play up-bow staccato?
Write SOLO over a whole note.

The badness of a musical composition is directly proportional to the number of violas in it.

Maestro (to Horns): "Give us the F in tune!" Violist (to Maestro): "Please can we have the F-in' tune, too?"

What's the best recording of the Walton Viola Concerto?
"Music Minus One"

What do a viola and a lawsuit have in common?
Everyone is relieved when the case is closed.

cello

How do you get a cellist to play fortissimo?
Write "pp, espressivo."

How do you make a cello sound beautiful?
Sell it and buy a violin.

Bass

How do you make a double bass sound in tune?
Chop it up and make it into a xylophone.

A double bass player arrived a few minutes late for the first rehearsal of the local choral society's annual performance of Handel's *Messiah*. He picked up his instrument and bow, and turned his attention to the conductor. The conductor asked, "Would you like a moment to tune?" The bass player replied with some surprise, "Why? Isn't it the same as last year?"

At a rehearsal, the conductor stops and shouts to the bass section: "You are out of tune. Check it, please! The first bassist pulls all his strings, says, "Our tuning is correct: all the strings are equally tight. The first violist turns around and shouts, "You bloody idiot! It's not the tension. The pegs have to be parallel!"

Two bass players were engaged for a run of Carmen. After a couple of weeks, they each agreed to take an afternoon off in turn to go watch the matinee performance from the front of the house. Joe duly took his break and watched the performance. Back in the pit that evening, Moe asked how it was. "Great," says Joe. "You know that bit where the music goes 'BOOM, Boom, boom, boom'? Well, there are some guys up top singing a terrific song about a Toreador at the same time."

There was a certain bartender who was quite famous for being able to accurately guess people's IQs. One night a man walked in and talked to him briefly and the bartender said, "Wow! You must have an IQ of about 140! You should meet this guy over here." So, they talked for a while about nuclear physics and existential philosophy and had a great time.

A second man walked in and soon the bartender has guessed about a 90 IQ for him. So, he sat him down in front of the big-screen TV and he watched football with the other guys and had a hell of a time.

Then a third man stumbled in and talked to the bartender for a while. The bartender said to himself, "Jeez! I think this guy's IQ must be about 29!" He took him over to a man sitting at a little table back in the corner and said, "You might enjoy talking with this guy for a while."

After the bartender left, the man at the table said, "So do you play French bow or German bow?"

Piano / Organ

Bob Hill and his new wife, Betty, are vacationing in Europe, and as it happens, in Transylvania. They're driving a rental car along a rather deserted highway. It's late, and raining very hard. Bob can barely see 10 feet in front of the car. Suddenly the car skids out of control! Bob attempts to control the car, but to no avail. The car swerves and smashes into a tree.

Moments later, Bob shakes his head to clear the fog. Dazed, he looks over at the passenger seat and sees his new wife unconscious, with her head bleeding. Despite the rain and unfamiliar countryside, Bob knows he has to carry her to the nearest phone. Bob carefully picks his wife up and begins trudging down the road. After a short while, he sees a light.

He heads towards the light, which is coming from an old, large house. He approaches the door and knocks. A minute passes. A small, hunched man opens the door. Bob immediately blurts, "Hello, my name is Bob Hill, and this is my wife, Betty. We've been in a terrible accident, and my wife has been seriously hurt. Can I please use your phone?"

"I'm sorry," replies the hunchback, "But we don't have a phone. My master is a doctor. Come in and I will get him."

Bob brings his wife in. An elegant man comes down the stairs. "I'm afraid my assistant may have misled you. I am not a medical doctor. I am a scientist. However, it is many miles to the nearest clinic, and I have had basic medical training. I will see what I can do. Igor, bring them down to the laboratory."

With that, Igor picks up Betty and carries her downstairs, with Bob following closely. Igor places Betty on a table in the lab. Bob collapses from exhaustion and his own injuries; so, Igor places Bob on an adjoining table. After a brief examination, Igor's master looks worried. "Things are serious, Igor. Prepare a transfusion."

Igor and his master work feverishly, but to no avail. Bob and Betty are no more.

The Hills' deaths upset Igor's master greatly. Wearily, he climbs the steps to his conservatory, which houses his pipe organ. For it is here that he has always found solace. He begins to play, and a stirring, haunting melody fills the house.

Meanwhile, Igor is still in the lab tidying up. As the music fills the lab, his eyes catch movement. He notices the fingers on Betty's hand twitch. Stunned, he watches as Bob's arm begins to rise! He is further amazed as Betty sits straight up!

Unable to contain himself, he dashes up the stairs to the conservatory. He bursts in and shouts to his master:

You sure you want to know?
O.K. You asked for it....
Wait for it…
"Master, Master! The Hills are alive with the sound of music!"
(Ouch!!! ...sorry 'bout that one...)

What do you get when you drop a piano down a mineshaft?
A flat minor.

What do you get when you drop a piano on an army base?
A flat major.

Why is an 11-foot concert grand better than a studio upright?
Because it makes a much bigger kaboom when dropped over a cliff.

The audience at a piano recital was appalled when a telephone rang just off stage. Without missing a note the soloist glanced toward the wings and called, "If that's my agent, tell him I'm working!"

What does a German Hammond organist do in his life's most tender moments?
He puts his Leslie on "slow".

Flute / Piccolo

How do you get two piccolo players to play in perfect unison?
Shoot one.

    Two musicians are walking down the street, and one says to the other, "Who was that piccolo I saw you with last night?" The other replies, "That was no piccolo, that was my fife."

Harp

Why are harps like elderly parents?
Both are unforgiving and hard to get into and out of cars.

How long does a harp stay in tune?
About 20 minutes, or until someone opens a door.

What's the definition of a quartertone?
A harpist tuning unison strings.

Clarinet

What's the definition of "nerd?"
Someone who owns his own alto clarinet.

What do you call a bass clarinetist with half a brain?
Gifted.

OBoe / Bassoon

Why are oboists and bassoonists the only musicians who make their own reeds?
Because the other musicians have social lives.

What is a burning oboe good for?
Setting a bassoon on fire.

Why is a bassoon better than an oboe?
The bassoon burns longer.

Why did the chicken cross the road?
To get away from the bassoon recital.

How do you put down a saxophone?
Call it a bassoon.

What's the difference between a bassoon and a trampoline?
You take off your shoes when you jump on a trampoline.

What is the definition of a half step?
Two oboes playing in unison.

What is the definition of a major second?
Two baroque oboes playing in unison.

How do you get an oboist to play A flat?
Take the batteries out of his electric tuner.

What's the difference between a SCUD missile and a bad oboist?
A bad oboist can kill you.

Saxophone

Before the 2001 inauguration of George Bush, he was invited to a get acquainted tour of the White House. After drinking several glasses of iced tea, he asked Bill Clinton if he could use his personal bathroom. When he entered Clinton's private toilet, he was astonished to see that President Clinton had a solid gold urinal. That afternoon, George told his wife, Laura, about the urinal. Just think, he said, when I am President, I could have a gold urinal too, but I wouldn't do something that self-indulgent! Later, when Laura had lunch with Hillary at her tour of the White House, she told Hillary how impressed George had been at his discovery of the fact, that in the President's private bathroom, the President had a golden urinal. That evening, when Bill and Hillary were getting ready for bed, Hillary smiled, and said to Bill, "I found out who pissed in your saxophone."

A warden is visiting Death Row. He walks up to a cell with two inmates in it. Warden says, "Now both you guys are gonna fry today, but you're each entitled to a last wish. What'll it be?" Inmate one says, "Sir, I just want to listen to my Kenny G. album all the way through." Warden says, "Well that sounds reasonable enough!" Then to inmate two he says, "Well, what about you? What's your last wish?" Inmate two says, "Kill me first!"

The soprano, not being smart enough to use birth control, says to her saxophonist lover, "Honey, I think you better pull out now." He replies, "Why? Am I sharp?"

What's the difference between a baritone saxophone and a chain saw?
The exhaust.

What's the difference between a saxophone and a lawn mower?
1. Lawn mowers sound better in a small ensemble.
2. The neighbors are upset if you borrow a lawn mower and don't return it.
3. The grip.
4. You can tune a lawn mower.

If you were lost in the woods, whom would you trust for directions: an in-tune tenor sax player, an out-of-tune tenor sax player, or Santa Claus?
The out-of-tune tenor sax player. The other two indicate you are hallucinating.

What's the difference between Kenny G and an Uzi machine gun?
The Uzi only repeats 200 times a minute.

How do you make a chain saw sound like a baritone sax?
Add vibrato.

One day Timmy came home from school very excited... "Mommy, Mommy, guess what? Today in English I got all the way to the end of the alphabet, and everyone else got messed up around 'P'!" His mother said, "Very good, dear. That's because you're a bari player." The next day, Timmy was even more excited. "Mommy, Mommy, guess what! Today in math I counted all the way to ten, but everyone else got messed up around seven!" "Very good, dear," his mother replied. "That's because you're a bari player." On the third day, Timmy was beside himself. "Mommy, Mommy, today we measured ourselves and I'm the tallest one in my class! Is that because I'm a bari player?"

"No dear," she said. "That's because you're 27 years old."

Why do sax players wear their neck straps around?
So they can get disability discounts.

What do a saxophone and a baseball have in common?
People cheer when you hit them with a bat.

You may be a redneck saxophonist if….
1. You have an old bass sax up on blocks in your yard.
2. You think the bell of your instrument is a great place to hold a longneck during a gig.
3. The gun rack on your pickup holds a couple of old sopranos.
4. You think that Boots Randolph is the greatest jazz musician who ever lived.

How To Play Saxophone

First things first: if you're a white guy, you'll need a stupid hat. The more stupid, the better and preferably a beret. Sunglasses are optional, but all the really, really good players wear them, especially indoors.

You'll also need some gig shirts - Hawaiians are good, but in a pinch, anything with a loud floral pattern is acceptable, as are T-shirts from various jazz clubs and festivals. The good thing about the latter is that you can get them mail order so you don't have to go to all the trouble of actually seeing and hearing live music. And sandals are an absolute must, even in winter.

Once you've assembled the proper attire, you can begin practicing. One of the most important things about playing is being able to convey emotion to the audience. This you do through various facial expressions.

The two emotions you'll need to convey are (1) rapture/ecstasy and (2) soul-wrenching pain and sadness (i.e. the blues). You may find it useful in the beginning to borrow a page from the method acting school.

So, for example, to convey rapture, try thinking of something nice-like puppy dogs or getting a rim job from Uma Thurman and then having her feed you mini hot dogs with truffle sauce.

To convey the "blues" try thinking of something really appalling- like ulcerative colitis or Alec Baldwin. You should practice your facial expressions in the mirror for at least two hours per day. You may feel a tad stupid at first, but you'll never get the chicks if you don't jump around on stage like a monkey - with your face screwed up like there's a rabid wolverine devouring your pancreas. And, bottom line, getting chicks is really what music is all about.

Next, you'll need the correct ligature. Some people think that the ligature is just a stupid old piece of metal that holds the reed on the mouthpiece. Well, those people are idiots. Besides your beret, the ligature is the single most important piece of musical equipment you will ever buy. Mine, for example, is 40% platinum and 60% titanium; one screw is rubidium and the other plutonium. It makes me sound exactly like Booker Ervin would, if Booker Ervin weren't (1) dead and/or (2) living on Mars. You may have to spend years and years and thousands of dollars finding the proper ligature, but in the end, it will definitely be worth it.

Now reeds. Optimally, you'll want to move to Cuba, grow and cure your own cane, and carve your own reeds by hand. If you're just a "weekend warrior" however, you can get by with the store-bought reeds. First, buy ten boxes of reeds - 100 in all. Next, open all the boxes and throw away 60 reeds. Take the remaining reeds and soak them in a mixture of 27.8% rubbing alcohol and 72.2% pituitary gland extract for a period of 17 weeks. Throw away 20 more reeds. Those were stuffy. Take the remaining 20 reeds and sand each one for exactly 13 seconds with #1200 grade 3M sandpaper. Throw away 14 reeds. Those squeaked. Take the remaining 6 reeds and soak them for another 17 weeks, this time however in a mixture of 27.8% pituitary gland extract and 72.2% rubbing alcohol. Sun dry the 6 remaining reeds for 3 weeks, optimally at an equatorial latitude, and throw away 3 more just on general principles. You now have 3 reeds that will last you several months if you play each one only 20 minutes a day in strict rotation.

You will also need some accouterments: a flight case capable of withstanding atmospheric pressure of $dP = -Dg\, dz$ where D and G are, respectively, the density of air and the acceleration due to gravity at the altitude of the air layer and dz is a horizontal layer of air having unit surface area and infinitesimal thickness; a metronome; a tuner; a combination alto-tenor-baritone sax stand with pegs for an oboe, bass clarinet, flute, English horn and bassoon; Band in a Box; a reed cutter; swabs, cleaners, pad savers, pad dope, pad clamps; a Sennheiser Digital Wireless Microphone; an effects rig with digital delay and parametric EQ; and a 200 watt (per channel, minimum) amplifier and 18" monitors.

It will be helpful if you listen to lots of sax players. Unfortunately, listening solely to players you like is absolutely the worst thing you can do. To really understand the music and its traditions you have to go back to the beginning and listen to every bit of music ever recorded. I'd start with madrigals and work forward. Once you get to the 20th century, pay particular attention to players like Jimmy Dorsey, Sidney Bechet, and Kenny G, who are the foundations of the modern jazz saxophone. In no time at all, or by 2034, whichever comes first, you'll be able to understand the unique be bop stylings of players like Ace Cannon, Boots Randolph and Sam Butera.

Finally, to play the sax itself, blow in the small end and move your fingers around.

A senile old man started walking through town every day in hopes of seeing interesting new things. On the first day, he saw a restaurant offering elephant ear sandwiches. He said to himself, "That's interesting. I'll go back home now." The next day, he walked along and suddenly found a dog that swallowed a cow in one gulp. "That's enough for today," he said. The very next day, he heard strangely melodic, low pitched music. He slowly walked around the corner and found a tenor sax player practicing. He said to himself, "Okay Harold, you need to go home now. Too much excitement has you hallucinating!"

A saxophonist comes home late from a gig... Too tired to carry her sax upstairs, she decides to leave it in the car for the night. When she wakes up she heads to her car only to see the back window smashed in. When she looks inside she sees two saxes.

A man has been trapped on an island for several years when he sees a small wake in the water. After a time, a lovely lady scuba diver rises from the surf. She walks to the man and exclaims, "You must be miserable, how long has it been since you have had a great smoke?" While the deranged man stammered for an answer, the lovely lady unzips the side pocket on her sleeve, and produces a Cuban cigar. She gazes into the now-smoking man's face and whispers, "And how long has it been since you have had a real drink?" Again, the man stammers as she unzips her other sleeve to produce a flask of ancient Brandy. As she teasingly unzips the main zipper to her wetsuit, she asks, "And how long has it been since you have known real pleasure?" The man scrambles to his feet and yells, "Oh my gosh, you don't really have a SAXOPHONE in there do ya?"

Small wonder we have so much trouble with air pollution in the world when so much of it has passed through saxophones.

Trumpet

The trumpet player drove up to the recording studio in a brand-new Mercedes Benz 500 SEL. The record producer said in astonishment, "You own that car? But you're only a trumpet player!" The quick-witted trumpet player replied, "Yeah, but I play flugelhorn, too."

(Alan Rubin, 1943—2011)

William Vacchiano (Manhattan School of Music) was big on teaching trumpet students to transpose various parts for variously pitched trumpet parts. Apparently, Miles Davis studied briefly with Vacchiano in the 1950's. During one lesson Vacchiano asked Miles: "If the piano is in the key of E, where does that put the trumpet?" Miles replied, "Back in the fucking case!"

The New York Philharmonic Orchestra, with Herbert Von Karian conducting, was about to begin rehearsal for the new season. One of the pieces features jazz trumpet in the fourth movement. Von Karian has threatened to quit.

He tells the Orchestra Board of Directors, "I will not work with a jazz musician. They are drunken, unwashed, use drugs and are completely unprofessional."

They finally convinced him to try it, so the morning of the first rehearsal, the musician's union sends over a man in a black beret, black sunglasses, black turtleneck sweater, sandals, and a beat-up trumpet in a brown paper bag.

The Fourth movement comes and this man is perfect. He plays like an angel. Von Karian is too embarrassed to even speak to him. This goes on for two weeks of rehearsals.

Now, it's the last session before opening night. The trumpet player has gotten even better and plays so beautifully the entire orchestra sheds tears of joy. They stand up and applaud him, hitting their bows on their strings. Von Karian is choked up. He goes to the man and embraces him saying, "I never liked jazz or jazz players, but you have changed my mind. You came every day on time, your tone and timing was perfect. You have inspired us all. I have never seen playing like that in my life."

The trumpet player says, "Well, it's the least I can do, considering I can't make the gig."

Trumpet #1: "Two weeks ago my aunt passed away and left me 12 million dollars."

Trumpet #2: "Wow man, that's great!"

Trumpet #1: "Yeah, then last week I won the lottery, three million bucks."

Trumpet #2: "That's excellent man, wow!"

Trumpet #1: Shrugs and says, "Yeah, but this week - - nothing."

In an emergency, a jazz trumpeter was hired to do some solos with a symphony orchestra. Everything went fine through the first movement, when she had some really hair-raising solos, but in the second movement she started improvising madly when she wasn't supposed to play at all. After the concert was over the conductor came around looking for an explanation. She said, "I looked in the score and it said 'tacit', so I took it!"

What's the difference between trumpet players and government bonds?
Government bonds eventually mature and earn money.

How do trumpet players traditionally greet each other?
"Hi. I'm better than you."

How do you know when a trumpet player is at your door?
The doorbell shrieks!

Why can't a gorilla play trumpet?
He's too sensitive.

What's the difference between a trumpet player and the rear end of a horse?
I don't know either.

What's the difference between a jet airplane and a trumpet?
About three decibels.

How many trumpet players does it take to pave a driveway?
Seven- if you lay them out correctly.

How are trumpet players like pirates?
They're both murder on the high Cs.

This trumpet player was on the phone with his agent. He was concerned that he hadn't had a gig in a while. His agent tells him; "Listen, there aren't any gigs out there, but I found you something. I got you a gig bagging lions."

To which the trumpet player says, "What does that have to do with my playing?" The agent then says, "Look, the gig pays a hundred dollars for each lion that you bag. Don't worry about playing."

At this point the trumpet player will take anything so he hangs up and flies to Africa. Not wanting to miss any practice time he takes his trumpet with him while looking for the lions. He notices a lion coming toward him and the only thing that he could think of doing is playing his horn.

He starts to play a beautiful ballad. He then notices that the lion starts to get sleepy and eventually goes to sleep. He grabs the lion, bags him and throws him in the back of his truck. He goes a little further and sees another lion. Again, he plays a beautiful ballad and again the lion falls asleep. This goes on all afternoon.

The trumpet player has about 99 lions in his truck when he sees another. He says, "What the heck, one more won't hurt." He starts to play his ballad and notices that the lion is not paying any attention to him so he starts to play louder. The lion starts to run toward the trumpet player. The trumpet player starts to play faster and faster but the lion keeps coming toward him. The lion jumps on the trumpet player and eats him.

One of the lions on the truck turns to another lion and says, "I told you that when he gets to the deaf one the gig would be over."

TromBone

Trombone Audition
Chicago Symphony Orchestra
Selection Committee
220 S. Michigan Avenue
Chicago, Illinois

Gentlemen:

I wish to apply immediately for the job of Second Trombone and I already have the two trombones. Although I have not played much in an orchestra, I have played along with lots of classic (no vocal) records. I found that if I slowed them down a little, the songs automatically went into the flat keys, which are much easier, but I think I could do the sharp keys in a short time.

I was a student for several years of Mr. Remington (Buck, not Emory) and then joined the circus band where my tone really got great. You don't have to worry about my being able to blast through on the Wagner stuff, that's for sure.

After I watched "10," I got out my horn and worked up a really great solo on "Bolero." (Do you know that there is a dance by this name too?) Does your arrangement sound the same all the way through, too? I still have trouble knowing when to come in with the record, though. Anyway, I know that if I get the job that the people in Chicago will like my version, which is do-wop.

Would I have to sit real close to the violins? They never seem to play very loud, and my tone sort of cuts off if I have to play too soft. It would be best if I could sit in front of the drums, like in the circus band. Also, I'd kind of like to sit on the outside so that people could see me.

I am practicing every day for the audition and am working on a new thing called legato, but it's still a little smeary. I think you'll like it though.

But, if your music is anything like this Rubank stuff, it will be a challenge to my teck... techininuque... tequch... ability. There is a position on trombones called 5th, but hardly any notes are there. Does your music have many of these notes, and if so, what are they? I'd like to know all of this before I pay bus fare down to Chicago.

How much does the job pay?

I'm really looking forward to coming down, but tell me why would I have to play behind a screen in the winter?

Sincerely,
Slide Rafferty

P.S. I have lots of music stands and probably have one like you guys use, so that would be cost saving.

What do you call a beautiful woman on a trombonist's arm?
A tattoo.

What kind of calendar does a trombonist use for his gigs?
"Year-At-A-Glance."

How do you know when a trombone player is at your door?
The doorbell drags.

What's the difference between a bass trombone and a chain saw?
1. Vibrato, though you can minimize this difference by holding the chain saw very still.
2. It's easier to improvise on a chain saw.

How can you make a French horn sound like a trombone?
1. Take your hand out of the bell and lose all sense of taste.
2. Take your hand out of the bell and miss all of the notes!

How do you know when there's a trombonist at your door?
His hat say's "Domino's."

What's the difference between a dead snake in the road and a dead trombonist in the road?
Skid marks in front of the snake.

What is the difference between a dead trombone player lying in the road, and a dead squirrel lying in the road?
The squirrel might have been on his way to a gig.

How do you improve the aerodynamics of a trombonist's car?
Take the Domino's Pizza sign off the roof.

What's the difference between a dead trombonist in the road and a dead country singer in the road?
The country singer may have been on the way to a recording session.

How can you tell which kid on a playground is the child of a trombonist?
He doesn't know how to use the slide, and he can't swing.

What is the dynamic range of the bass trombone?
On or off.

What is another term for trombone?
A wind driven, manually operated, pitch approximator.

It is difficult to trust anyone whose instrument changes shape as he plays it!

French Horn

A girl went out on a date with a trumpet player, and when she came back her roommate asked, "Well, how was it? Did his embouchure make him a great kisser?" "Nah," the first girl replied. "That dry, tight, tiny little pucker was no fun at all." The next night she went out with a tuba player, and when she came back her roommate asked, "Well, how was his kissing?" "Ugh!" the first girl exclaimed. "Those huge, rubbery, blubbery, slobbering slabs of meat were just gross!" The next night she went out with a French horn player, and when she came back her roommate asked, "Well, how was his kissing?" "Well," the first girl replied, "His kissing was just so-so; but I *loved* the way he held me!"

There once was a woman who had gone a long time without so much as a hope of having a relationship. When she finally picked up a handsome looking guy and went out with him, her friends were naturally curious as to how it went. "What's he like?" said the woman's friend the day after the big event. "Oh, he's fine, I guess. He's a musician, you know," said she. "Does he have class?" said the friend. The friend's ears perked up as the woman said, "Well, most of the time, yes, but I don't think I'll be going out with him again." "Oh? Why not?" asked the friend. "Well, he plays the French horn, so I guess it's just a habit, but every time we kiss, he sticks his fist up my ass!"

What do you get when you cross a French horn player and a goalpost?
A goalpost that can't march.

What's the difference between a French horn and a weather report?
The weather report is more accurate.

How can you make a trombone sound like a French horn?
Stick your hand in the bell and play a lot of wrong notes.

Why is the French horn a divine instrument?
Because man blows into it, but only God knows what comes out of it.

How do you get your viola section to sound like the horn section?
Have them miss every other note.

TuBa

What's the range of a tuba?
Twenty yards if you've got a good arm!

What's a tuba for?
1 1/2" by 3 1/2" unless you request "full cut."
   Note: in the USA, a 2 x 4 is a two-inch by four-inch piece of wood, which actually measures 1 1/2 inches by 3 1/2 inches.

How do you fix a broken tuba?
With a tuba glue.

These two tuba players walk past a bar...
Well, it *could* happen!

Accordion

What's the definition of an optimist?
An accordion player with a pager.

"Use an Accordion... Go to Jail!" (bumper sticker)

What's an accordion good for?
Learning how to fold a map.

What's a bassoon good for?
Kindling for an accordion fire.

What's the difference between an Uzi and an accordion?
The Uzi stops after 20 rounds.

If you drop an accordion, a set of bagpipes and a viola off a twenty-story building, which one lands first?
Who cares?

Do you know what the difference between an accordion and a trampoline?
You take your shoes off to jump on a trampoline!

What do you call ten accordions at the bottom of the ocean?
A good start.

What's the definition of a gentleman?
One who knows how to play the accordion, but doesn't.

What do you call a group of topless female accordion players?
Ladies in Pain.

For three years, the young accordion player had been taking his brief vacations at the same country inn. The last time, he'd finally managed to have an affair with the innkeeper's daughter. Looking forward to an exciting few days, he dragged his suitcase up the stairs of the inn, and then stopped short. There sat his lover with an infant on her lap! "Darling, why didn't you write when you learned you were pregnant?" he cried. "I would have rushed up here, we could have gotten married, and the baby would have my name!" "Well," she said, "When my folks found out about my condition, we sat up all night talking and decided it would be better to have a bastard in the family than an accordion player."

SHE TRIED TO BE GOOD, BUT KNEW SHE COULDN'T RESIST THE SHACK AND FALLING UNDER THE SPELL OF THE

REBEL WITH AN ACCORDION

Accordion to a recent study, 7 out of 10 people don't notice when a word in a sentence is replaced by a musical instrument.

Banjo

What's the difference between a banjo and a chain saw?
The chain saw has greater dynamic range.

What's the least-used sentence in the English language?
"Isn't that the banjo player's Porsche?"

How are a banjo player and a blind javelin thrower alike?
Both command immediate attention and alarm and force everyone to move out of range.

There's nothing I like better than the sound of a banjo, unless, of course, it's the sound of a chicken caught in a vacuum cleaner.

I recently was told I needed surgery on my hand, and I asked the doctor if after surgery I would be able to play the banjo. "I'm operating on your hand, not giving you a lobotomy!"

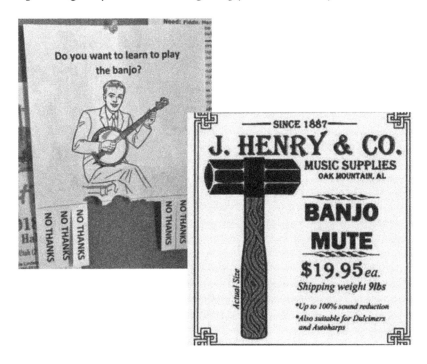

Say What?

"If music be the food of love, play on."

—William Shakespeare

"When I think about kids watching a TV show like American Idol or The Voice, then they think, "Oh, OK, that's how you become a musician, you stand in line for eight fucking hours with 800 people at a convention center and then you sing your heart out for someone and then they tell you it's not fuckin' good enough. Can you imagine? It's destroying the next generation of musicians! Musicians should go to a yard sale and buy an old fucking drum set and get in their garage and just suck. And get their friends to come in and they'll suck, too. And then they'll fucking start playing and they'll have the best time they've ever had in their lives and then all of a sudden, they'll become Nirvana. Because that's exactly what happened with Nirvana.

Just a bunch of guys that had some shitty old instruments and they got together and started playing some noisy-ass shit, and they became the biggest band in the world. That can happen again! You don't need a fucking computer or the Internet or The Voice or American Idol."

—Dave Grohl

"Canned music is like audible wallpaper."

—Alistair Cooke

"These days, what isn't worth saying is sung."

—Pierre De Beaumarchais

"Song: the licensed medium for bawling in public things too silly or sacred to be uttered in ordinary speech."

—Oliver Herford

"Good music resembles something. It resembles the composer."

—Jean Cocteau

"Hell is full of musical amateurs."

—George Bernard Shaw

"Listen kid, take my advice, never hate a song that has sold half a million copies."

—Irving Berlin to Cole Porter

"Sang like a hinge."

—Ethel Merman on Cole Porter

"I prefer neurotic people. I like to hear rumblings beneath the surface."

—Stephen Sondheim

"If true computer music were ever written, it would only be listened to by other computers."

—Michael Crichton

"I think popular music in this country is one of the few things in the twentieth century that have made giant strides in reverse."

—Bing Crosby

"The reason we have lasted so long is that we play music for lovers rather than acrobats."

—Guy Lombardo

"I don't know anything about music. In my line, you don't have to."

—Elvis Presley

"I hang my laundry on the line when I write."

—Joni Mitchell

"SOMETIMES IT'S TO YOUR ADVANTAGE FOR PEOPLE TO THINK YOU'RE CRAZY"

Thelonious Monk

"Do you know the difference between education and experience? Education is when you read the fine print; experience is what you get when you don't."

—Pete Seeger

"I can hold a note as long as the Chase Manhattan Bank."

—Ethel Merman

"Being a lounge act at the Union Plaza is as close to being out of show business as you can get."

—Maynard Sloate (former Entertainment Director—Union Plaza Hotel, Las Vegas)

"I hand him a lyric and get out of his way."

—Oscar Hammerstein on Richard Rogers

"I have long harbored a suspicion that most country songwriters moonlight as speech writers for President Reagan or scriptwriters for "Dallas," since they share a desire to reduce all life to the dimensions of a B-movie."

—Paul Lasher

"We are buried beneath the weight of information, which is being confused with knowledge; quantity is being confused with abundance and wealth with happiness.

We are monkeys with money and guns.

— Tom Waits

"Yeah, country music."
>—Buddy Rich (on his death bed, when asked by an attending nurse about to give him a hypodermic, "Mr. Rich, are you allergic to anything?")

"I was banging my head against a shower stall wall and I wasn't in time."
>—Buddy Rich (in response to Don Piestrip's question at the end, "When did you know you were sick, Buddy?")

"I intend to put the "cunt" back in country music."
>—Rosalind Cash

"Rock 'n' Roll is part of a pest to undermine the morals of the youth of our nation. It is sexualistic, unmoralistic, and…brings people of both races together."
>—North Alabama's White Citizen Council

"The success of today's rock songs proves one thing—rhyme doesn't pay."

—Earl Wilson

"On stage I make love to 25,000 people; then I go home alone."

—Janis Joplin

"You have to be a bastard to make it, and that's a fact. And the Beatles are the biggest bastards on earth. When we say 'War is over if you want it,' we mean if everyone demanded peace instead of another TV set, we'd have peace."

—John Lennon

"Lots of people who complained about us receiving the MBE received theirs for heroism in the war—for killing people. We received ours for entertaining other people. I'd say we deserve ours more."

—John Lennon

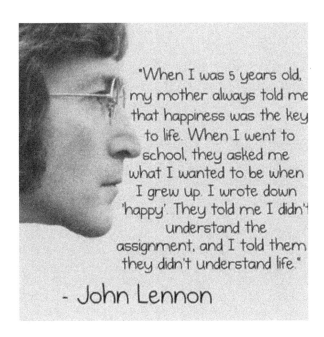

"When I was 5 years old, my mother always told me that happiness was the key to life. When I went to school, they asked me what I wanted to be when I grew up. I wrote down 'happy'. They told me I didn't understand the assignment, and I told them they didn't understand life."

- John Lennon

"If there is such a thing as genius, which is just what—what the fuck is?—I am one, you know. And if there isn't, I don't care."
—John Lennon

"I was appalled when the San Francisco ethic didn't mushroom and envelop the whole world into this loving community of acid freaks. I was very naïve."
—Grace Slick

"I'm into pop because I want to get rich, get famous, and get laid."
—Bob Geldof

"When you're a rock star, you're allowed to be a petulant child and many other things you're supposed to grow out of."
—Sting

"I'm the Connie Francis of rock and roll."
—Elton John

"A lot of fellows nowadays have a B.A., M.D., or Ph.D. Unfortunately, they don't have a J.O.B."
—"Fats" Domino

"I bit the head off a bat the other night. It was like eating a crunchie wrapped in chamois leather."
—Ozzy Osborne

"I'd rather be dead than sing "Satisfaction" when I'm 45."
—Mick Jagger

"I'm a rock star because I couldn't be a soccer star."
—Rod Stewart

"The last thing I wanted to do was have a fist fight with Pete Townshend. Unfortunately, he hit me first with a guitar."
—Roger Daltry

> "Music to me is like breathing –
> I don't get tired of breathing,
> I don't get tired of
> music."
>
> Ray Charles

"That dead son-of-a-bitch is still riding on my coattails."
— Jerry Lee Lewis (about Elvis Presley)

"After I die, I shall return to earth as a gatekeeper of a bordello and I won't let any of you—not one of you—enter!"
— Arturo Toscanini (castigating a less than proficient orchestra)

"I occasionally play works by contemporary composers for two reasons. First to discourage the composer from writing any more and secondly to remind myself how much I appreciate Beethoven."
— Jascha Heifitz

"If I don't practice one day, I know it; two days, the critics know it; three days, the public knows it."
— Jascha Heifitz

"No matter which side of an argument you're on, you always find some people on your side that you wish were on the other side."

—Jascha Heifitz

"The fact that people do not understand and respect the very best things, such as Mozart's concertos, is what permits men like us to become famous."

—Johannes Brahms

"Sometimes I think, not so much am I a pianist, but a vampire. All my life I have lived off the blood of Chopin."

—Arturo Rubenstein

"I don't believe in tradition. It is a form of laziness."

—Leopold Stokowski

"If everything would be permitted to me, I would feel lost in this abyss of freedom."

—Igor Fedorovich Stravinsky

"The seasons…are authentic; there is no mistake about them, they are what a symphony ought to be: four perfect movements in intimate harmony with one another."

—Arthur Rubinstein

"When a piece gets difficult, make faces."
                                    —Arthur Schnabel to Vladimir Horowitz

"He was the only pianist I have ever seen who did not grimace. That is a great deal."
                                    —Igor Stravinsky on Sergei Rachmaninov

"There are some composers—at the head of whom stands Beethoven—who not only do not know when to stop but appear to stop many times before they actually do."
                                    —Virginia Graham

"I write as a sow piddles."
                                    —Wolfgang Amadeus Mozart

"I don't want anyone to admire my pants in a museum."
                                    —Frederic Chopin

"My God—who do they think I am—everybody?"
                                    Leonard Bernstein (feeling the pressure of too many people wanting his ear)

"You know whatta you do when you shit? Singing, it's the same thing, only up!"
                                    —Enrico Caruso

"Playing 'bop' is like playing Scrabble with all the vowels missing."
                                    —Duke Ellington

"I'll play it first and tell you what it is later."
                                    —Miles Davis

"I can't stand to sing the same song the same way two nights in succession. If you can, then it ain't music, it's a close order drill, or exercise or yodeling, or something, not music."
                                    —Billy Holiday

"A lot of cats copy the Mona Lisa, but people still line up to see the original."

    —Louis Armstrong (when asked if he minded performers imitating his style)

"I stole from everything I ever heard, but mostly I stole from the horns."

    —Ella Fitzgerald

"Women, horses, cars, clothes. I did it all. And do you know what that's called? It's called living."

    —Cab Calloway

"Anybody singing the blues is in a deep pit yelling for help."

    —Mahalia Jackson

"Audiences like their blues singers to be miserable."

—Janis Joplin

"Jazz will endure just as long as people hear it through their feet instead of their brains."

—John Philip Sousa

"Jazz music was invented by demons for the torture of imbeciles."

—Henry Van Dyke

"This particularly rapid, unintelligible patter isn't generally heard, and if it is it doesn't matter!"

—W.S. Gilbert (discussing disc jockeys)

"Radio news is bearable. This is due to the fact that while the news is being broadcast, the disc jockey is not allowed to talk."
—Fran Lebowitz

"The wriggling ponces of the spoken word."
—D.G. Bridson (on disc jockeys)

"My choice early in life was either to be a piano player in a whorehouse or a politician. And to tell the truth, there's hardly any difference."
—Harry Truman

"I'm making six bills a week: a twenty, a ten, two fives and two ones."
—Dick Berk

"Without music to decorate it, time is just a bunch of boring production deadlines or dates by which bills must be paid."
—Frank Zappa

"In the beginning was the note, and the note was with God; and whosoever can reach for that note, reach high, and bring it back to us on earth…to the extent of his reach, partakes of the divine…."
—Leonard Bernstein

"I tried making a living and that didn't work. So, fuck it, I became a Producer. I feel much better."
—Carl Rosenberg

"When it comes to racing into any new technology, the record business finishes just ahead of the Amish."
—Stan Cornyn

"Be so good they can't ignore you."
—Steve Martin

"Those who dance are considered insane by those who cannot hear the music."

—George Carlin

"Music is my religion."

—Jimi Hendrix

"Musicians aren't real people."

—Lucy (off and on girlfriend of Linus)

"I think there must be a music school someplace where musicians go to learn harmony, counterpoint and sarcasm!"

—Lucy (off and on girlfriend of Linus)

"An average band with a great drummer sounds great.
A great band with an average drummer sounds average."

—Buddy Rich

"I can't understand why people are frightened of new ideas. I'm frightened of the old ones."

—John Cage

"Technique doesn't mean shit if you can't play a backbeat and lock it in."

—Steve Gadd

"Because I think I'm making progress."
  —Pablo Casals (when the legendary cellist was asked why he continued to practice at age 90.)

"Music is what I am. Everything else is what I do."
  —All of us

"My grandkids always beat me at Rock Band. And I say, 'You may beat me at Rock Band, but I made the original records, so shut up.'"

—Paul McCartney

"I don't understand these kids auditioning for X-Factor claiming they 'Just wanna make music.' Cut the crap! Let me introduce you to the kid teaching himself how to play guitar, or the busker in the train station, or the guys and girls recording their own demos and playing the small venues, or the unpublished songwriter with countless books full of lyrics, or the people who just want to be heard, who want to express themselves, their creativity and their artistic vision. They are the ones who just want to make music! They are the real artists! Anybody auditions for X-Factor it's because they want to be famous! Period! Otherwise they'd already be out there 'making music.'"

—Bruce Dickinson (Frontman of Iron Maiden)

"I never play it the same way once."

—Shelly Manne

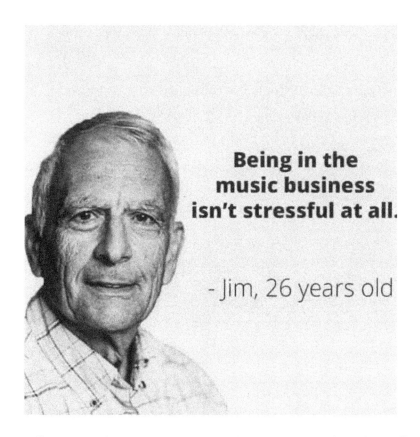

Being in the music business isn't stressful at all.

- Jim, 26 years old

"Listen to the stage manager and get on stage when they tell you to. No one has the time for the rockstar bullshit. None of the techs backstage care if you are David Bowie or the milkman. When you act like a jerk, they are completely unimpressed with the infantile display that you might think comes with your dubious status. They were there hours before you, building the stage, and they will be there hours after you leave, tearing it down. They should get your salary and you should get theirs."

—Henry Rollins

"I would teach children music, physics, and philosophy; but most importantly music, for the patterns in music and all the arts are the keys to learning."

—Plato

"My sole inspiration is a telephone call from a producer."
—Cole Porter

"Don't bother to look, I've composed all this already."
—Gustav Mahler (To Bruno Walter who had stopped to admire mountain scenery in rural Austria.)

"I would rather play Chiquita Banana and have my swimming pool than play Bach and starve."
—Xavier Cugat

"Musicians talk of nothing but money and jobs. Give me businessmen every time. They really are interested in music and art."
—Jean Sibelius (Explaining why he rarely invited musicians to his home.)

"The amount of money one needs is terrifying..."
—Ludwig van Beethoven

"Only become a musician if there is absolutely no other way you can make a living."
—Kirke Mecham (On his life as a composer.)

"Chaos is a friend of mine."
—Bob Dylan

"There is nothing more difficult than talking about music."
—Camille Saint-Sans

"I am not handsome, but when women hear me play, they come crawling to my feet."
—Niccoli Paganini

"Of course, I'm ambitious. What's wrong with that? Otherwise you sleep all day."
—Ringo Starr

"What is the voice of song, when the world lacks the ear of taste?"
—Nathaniel Hawthorne

"Flint must be an extremely wealthy town. I see that each of you bought two or three seats.
—Victor Borge (Playing to a half-filled house in Flint, Michigan.)

"If one hears bad music, it is one's duty to drown it by one's conversation."
—Oscar Wilde

"Critics can't even make music by rubbing their back legs together."
—Mel Brooks

"Life can't be all bad when, for ten dollars, you can buy all the Beethoven sonatas and listen to them for ten years."
—William F. Buckley, Jr.

"You can't possibly hear the last movement of Beethoven's Seventh and go slow."
—Oscar Levant (Explaining his way out of a speeding ticket.)

"Wagner's music is better than it sounds."
—Mark Twain

"I love Beethoven, especially the poems."
—Ringo Starr

"Berlioz says nothing in his music, but he says it magnificently."
—James Gibbons Hunekar

"If a young man at the age of twenty-three can write a symphony like that, in five years he will be ready to commit murder."

—Walter Damrosch (On Aaron Copland.)

"There are still so many beautiful things to be said in C major."

—Sergei Prokofiev

"I never use a score when conducting my orchestra... Does a lion tamer enter a cage with a book on how to tame a lion?"

—Dimitri Mitropolous

"God tells me how the music should sound, but you stand in the way."

—Arturo Toscanini (To a trumpet player.)

"Already too loud!"

—Bruno Walter (At his first rehearsal with an American orchestra, on seeing the players reaching for their instruments.)

"Movie music is noise. It's even more painful than my sciatica."

—Sir Thomas Beecham

"Theirs [the Beatles] is a happy, cocky, belligerently resourceless brand of harmonic primitivism... In the Liverpudlian repertoire, the indulgent amateurishness of the musical material, though closely rivaled by the indifference of the performing style, is actually surpassed only by the ineptitude of the studio production method. (Strawberry Fields suggests a chance encounter at a mountain wedding between Claudio Monteverdi and a jug band.)"

—Glenn Gould

"It's pretty clear now that what looked like it might have been some kind of counterculture is, in reality, just the plain old chaos of undifferentiated weirdness."

—Jerry Garcia

"In opera, there is always too much singing."

—Claude Debussy

"An exotic and irrational entertainment.

—Samuel Johnson (His definition of opera.)

"If a thing isn't worth saying, you sing it."

—Pierre Beaumarchais

"The Barber of Seville Opera is where a guy gets stabbed in the back, and instead of dying, he sings."

—Robert Benchley

"I'd hate this to get out, but I really like opera."

—Ford Frick

"Oh, how wonderful, really wonderful opera would be if there were no singers!"

—Gioacchino Rossini

"Never look at the trombones. It only encourages them."

—Richard Strauss

"I really don't know whether any place contains more pianists than Paris, or whether you can find more asses and virtuosos anywhere."

—Frederic Chopin

"When she started to play, Steinway himself came down personally and rubbed his name off the piano."

—Bob Hope (On comedienne Phyllis Diller.)

"Nine AM reminds me of Tommy Dorsey at MGM many years ago. The assistant director told Tommy that he and his band were to be in makeup at eight o'clock the next day, in order to be ready by nine. They were being featured in "DuBarry Was a Lady," one of MGM's top musicals, with Lucy and Red Skelton co-starring. Dorsey asked the assistant, 'You mean eight o'clock in the morning?' 'Of course,' he was told. 'Jesus Christ,' said Dorsey, 'My boys don't even start vomiting till eleven.'"

—Desi Arnaz

An old trumpet player says to a young trumpet player, "The good news is you've got a great technique. The bad news is you've got a great technique."

—Bob Barnard

"All I wanted was to be big, to be in show business, and to travel ... and that's what I've been doing all my life."

—Count Basie

"Brass bands are all very well in their place, outdoors and several miles away."

—Sir Thomas Beecham

"There are two golden rules for an orchestra: start together and finish together. The public doesn't give a damn what goes on in between."

—Sir Thomas Beecham

"The boppers flat their fifths. We consume ours."

—Eddie Condon

"Ted Lewis could make the clarinet talk. What it said was 'put me back in the case!'"

—Eddie Condon

"If you get your guitar in tune, send it to me and I'll send you mine."

—Herb Ellis (His ad in the "International Musician.")

"Muzak goes in one ear, and out some other opening."

Anton Kuerti (Austrian-born Canadian pianist.)

"Only sick music makes money today."

—Friederich Nietzsche

"Playing jazz for a living sure beats the hell out of stealing."

—John Sheridan

"For indie bands, the new publicity is no publicity."

—Jason Richards, The Atlantic

"I remember playing the guitar through the amplifier facing out the window of my house onto the street in the summer time—that was social media in 1992."

—John Meyer

Jazzed

(This was the winner of a recent Short Story Contest. The rules stipulated that the stories had to be 200 words or less with no profanity, and all anatomical references had to be replaced with musical instruments, players, or references to music.)

It was a balmy night out and I was feeling thelonious. I hadn't had any tatum in so long I could have bixed a choirgirl. But I wouldn't have to -- the moment I entered the Luboff Lounge, the babe with the giant eubies fixed me with a "come duke me" look. She uncrossed her legs and I could see almost all the way to birdland. I felt a tingle in my tito puente, and with a smile, I had her. This is it.

No sooner had we closed my front door than this hot django had grabbed me by the hines and pulled me close. I insinuated my hand under her sweater until I found one of her brubecks, then I slowly traced a circle around her lee konitz. "Oh, baby," she cooed, "You make my red norvo wet." She unzipped my getz, and reached in to cradle my johnny hodges in her hand. "I'd love a little mingus, darling. My gillespie is aching."

By this time my king oliver was ready to take a solo; I could hardly wait to coda, but I obliged her. She hoisted her skirt, and I saw that she wasn't wearing any basies. I dove right into her satchmo and attacked her lennie tristano. "Ooh," she moaned, "I want your krupa! Zoot me! Fill my cootie williams!"

I was ready -- almost. I felt in my pocket. Uh -- oh. "Sorry, sweets," I said. "No blakey tonight. I'm all out of condons."

Yogi Berra Explains Jazz

Interviewer: What do you expect is in store for the future of jazz guitar?

Yogi: I'm thinkin' there'll be a group of guys who've never met, talkin' about it all the time.

Interviewer: Can you explain jazz?

Yogi: I can't, but I will. 90% of all jazz is half improvisation. The other half is the part people play while others are playing something they never played with anyone who played that part. So, if you play the wrong part, it's right. If you play the right part, it might be right if you play it wrong enough. But if you play it too right, it's wrong.

Interviewer: I don't understand.

Yogi: Anyone who understands jazz knows that you can't understand it. It's too complicated. That's what's so simple about it.

Interviewer: Do you understand it?

Yogi: No. That's why I can explain it. If I understood it, I wouldn't know anything about it.

Interviewer: Are there any great jazz players alive today?

Yogi: No. All the great jazz players alive today are dead. Except for the ones that are still alive. But so many of them are dead, that the ones that are still alive are dying to be like the ones that are dead. Some would kill for it.

Interviewer: What is syncopation?

Yogi: That's when the note that you should hear now happens either before or after you hear it. In jazz, you don't hear notes when they happen because that would be some other type of music. Other types of music can be jazz, but only if they're the same as something different from those other kinds.

Interviewer: Now I really don't understand.

Yogi: I haven't taught you enough for you to not understand jazz that well.

The Evil Spell

A frog jumping out of the bushes onto the road startles two attractive young ladies walking down a country lane.

They are even more surprised when the frog assumes a theatrical pose and begins to speak Frog (in Shakespearean tones): "O ye fair damsels, what ye see before ye is not really an ugly frog, but a jazz musician that was transformed into a frog by the evil spell of a wicked witch. But, if one of ye beautiful maidens is brave enough to kiss me, the evil spell will be broken, and I will be transformed back into a great jazz musician. For, before the witch's spell turned me into a slimy frog, I was the greatest jazz musician that ever lived!"

For a moment, the two young ladies are dumbfounded and stand staring at the frog in amazement. Suddenly, one of the girls quickly snatches up the frog and puts it in her pocket. "Well, aren't you going to kiss it then?" asks her friend. "Are you kidding?" says the first. "A talking frog is worth a hell of a lot more than a jazz musician."

Define "Jazz Musician"

A Jazz musician is someone that puts a $5,000 horn in a $500 car and drives 50 miles for a $5 gig.

I'm all in favor of getting Grants for jazz musicians -- or any other good brand of Scotch.

"If you really want to communicate something, even if it's just an emotion or an attitude, let alone an idea, the least effective and least enjoyable way is directly. It only goes in about an inch. But if you can get people to the point where they have to think a moment what it is you're getting at, and then discover it, the thrill of discovery goes right through the heart."

—Stanley Kubrick

I Need Some Advice!

Dear Abby,

I am an Airman stationed at Lackland AFB. My parents live in the suburbs of Philadelphia and one of my sisters, who lives in Bensonhurst, is married to a transvestite. My father and mother have recently been arrested for growing and selling marijuana and are currently dependent on my other two sisters, who are prostitutes in Jersey City.

I have two brothers, one who is currently serving a non-parole life sentence in Attica, for the rape & murder of a teenage boy in 1994, the other currently being held in the Wellington Remand Center on charges of incest with his three children.

I have recently become engaged to marry a former Thai prostitute who lives in the Bronx and indeed is still a part-time "working girl" in a brothel, however, her time there is limited, as she has recently been infected with an STD. We intend to marry as soon as possible and are currently looking into the possibility of opening our own brothel, with my fiancé utilizing her knowledge of the industry working as the manager.

I am hoping my two sisters would be interested in joining our team. Although I would prefer them not to prostitute themselves, at least it would get them off the streets and, hopefully, off the heroin.

I love my fiancé and look forward to bringing her into the family. Of course, I want to be totally honest with her, so, my problem is this: should I tell her about my cousin who is a jazz musician?

Signed,
Worried About My Reputation

Who says music doesn't pay?

Think you don't get paid enough for what you do?

Check out the pay sheet for one of the sessions that yielded half of Miles Davis' best-known album, *Kind of Blue*.

Davis was paid $129.36, while John Coltrane, Cannonball Adderly, Wynton Kelly and Bill Evans were paid $64.67.

Paul Chambers and Jimmy Cobb, on bass and drums respectively, were paid $66.67, the extra two dollars for "cartage" of their instrument.

No joke.

Know how to make a million dollars singing jazz?
Start with two million.

Two musicians are driving down a road. All of a sudden, they notice the Grim Reaper in the back seat. Death informs them that they had an accident and they both died. But, before he must take them off into eternity, he grants each musician one last request to remind them of their past life on earth. The first musician says he was a Country & Western musician and would like to hear eight choruses of *Achy-Breaky Heart* as a last hoorah! The second musician says "I was a jazz musician...kill me now!"

A Jazz musician was told by his doctor, "I am very sorry to tell you that you have cancer and you have only one more year to live." The Jazz musician replied, "And what am I going to live on for an entire year?"

Taken right from the Internet: A Great Jazz Opportunity (Is there such a thing?)
My name is Nodugood. I am a wealthy Nigerian prince who loves the jazz of music.

I am seeking your help to move $200,000,000 from my checking account here in Nigeria to the United States. I too love the jazz of music and am planning to flee to America to open many jazz clubs at which I would like you to perform.

You will receive $42,000 a night, plus a meal.

My new "Tribal Village Vanguard" clubs will be of great success and you will become rich like the rest of American jazz musicians.

I have already applied for building exemptions to allow thatched stages and the spearing of live animals. But I desperately need your help. My tribe, the Swindlisi, a peaceful jazz-loving people, has been horribly oppressed by the ruling military junta, which despises the jazz of music.

My father, an exiled king and booking agent, was recently imprisoned under the Draconian "three gigs - you're out" law, and now I must flee my beloved country with all of my improbable wealth - But I need help in moving it.

I have so much money that it will not fit in the allotted two checked bags and one carry-on. I am therefore wanting to transfer the money through your ATM system (The Nigerian ATM system cannot exchange international currencies; it only converts "antelope" to money.) So please to just provide me with your full name and address, social security number, bank account and PIN numbers, and you will become incredibly (literally) rich from playing many jazz gigs.

(Note: normal Nigerian Musician's Union rules apply: three hour performances, two 15 minute breaks allowed, musicians to provide their own mosquito nets, one open fire per bandstand, one free meal plus anything you kill.)

Act now. The first ten musicians to respond will receive a free copy of the Nigeria's Greatest Jazz Hits CD, by our beloved 'Disoriented' Gillespie Band, which contains the hits:

The Night Has A Thousand Flies
Goodbye Shrunken Head
Here's That Rainy Season
Just Tribesmen (Lovers No More)
Take the 'A' Trail
When I Fall In Quicksand
Half-Nelson Mandella
Blue Monkey
Leopard Skins and Moonbeams
Blue Mombossa
Almost Like Being In Lagos
Sunny Side of the Goatpath
I Didn't Know What Century It Was

Thank you for your many help.

Your inordinately wealthy Nigerian brother...
Prince Nodugood

Singin' The Blues

1. Most blues begin, "Woke up this morning."

2. "I got a good woman" is a bad way to begin the blues, unless you stick something nasty in the next line like, "I got a good woman, with the meanest dog in town."

3. Blues are simple. After you have the first line right, repeat it. Then find something that rhymes. Sort of. Like this, "Got a good woman with the meanest dog in town. He got teeth like Margaret Thatcher and he weigh 500 pound. (Subjects and verbs must not agree)."

4. The blues are not about limitless choice, convertible debentures, golden parachutes, BMWs, opera, or environmental impact statements. "You stuck in a ditch, you stuck in a ditch; ain't no way out." That's the blues.

5. Blues cars are Chevys and Cadillacs and broken-down trucks. Other acceptable blues transportation is a Greyhound

bus or a southbound train. Walkin' plays a major part in the blues lifestyle. So does fixin' to die.

6. Teenagers can't sing the Blues. They ain't fixin' to die yet. Adults sing the Blues. In Blues, "adulthood" means being old enough to get the electric chair if you shoot a man in Memphis.

7. You can have the blues in New York City, but not in Brooklyn or Queens. Hard times in Vermont or North Dakota are just a depression. Chicago, St. Louis, Austin and Kansas City are still the best places to have the blues. You cannot have the blues in any place that don't get rain.

8. The following colors do not belong in the blues:
    a. violet
    b. beige
    c. mauve
    d. taupe

9. You can't have no blues in an office or a shopping mall - the lighting is all wrong. Go outside to the parking lot - or sit by the dumpster.

10A. Good places for the Blues:
    a. The highway
    b. The jailhouse
    c. An empty bed

10B. Bad places for the blues:
    a. Ashrams
    b. Gallery openings
    c. Weekends in the Hamptons
    d. Trump Plaza

11. No one will believe it's the Blues if you wear a suit, unless you happen to be an old ethnic man and you slept in the suit.

12 A. Yes, it's the Blues if:
    a. Your first name is a southern state -- like Georgia.
    b. You're blind.
    c. You shot a man in Memphis (see exception below) .
    d. Your woman can't be satisfied.

12 B. No, it's not the Blues if:
    a. You were once blind but now can see.
    b. You have a trust fund.

c. You hold elected office.

d. Your woman CAN be satisfied.

13. Neither Julio Iglesias nor Barbara Streisand can sing the blues.

14A. If you ask for water and baby gives you gasoline, it's the blues.

Other blues beverages are:

a. Cheap wine

b. Irish whiskey

c. Muddy water

d. Black coffee

14B. Blues beverages are NOT:

a. Any mixed drink

b. Any Kosher wine for Passover

c. Yoo Hoo (all flavors)

d. Snapple

e. Sparkling water

15. If it occurs in a cheap motel or a shotgun shack, it's blues death. Stabbed in the back by a jealous lover is a blues way to die.

Other blues ways to die include:

a. The electric chair

b. Substance abuse

c. Being denied treatment in an emergency room

d. Dying lonely on a broken-down cot

It is NOT a blues death if you die during a tennis match or getting liposuction.

16A. Some Blues names for Women

a. Sadie

b. Big Mama

c. Bessie

d. Fat River Dumpling

16B. Some Blues Names for Men

a. Joe

b. Willie

c. Little Willie

d. Big Willie

e. Big Blind Willie

f. Fat Willie

g. Lightning

Persons with names like Sierra, Auburn, Rainbow or Sequoia will not be permitted to sing the blues no matter how many men they shoot in Memphis.

16C. Other Blues Names Must Include:

a. Name of physical infirmity (Blind, Cripple, Asthmatic)

b. First name (see above) or name of fruit (Lemon, Lime, Kiwi)

c. Last name of a dead President (Jefferson, Johnson, Fillmore, etc.)

For example, Blind Lemon Jefferson, Anorexic Willie, or Cripple Cherimoya. (Personally, I dig "Asthmatic Kiwi Fillmore" given the above choices...)

17. A man with male pattern baldness ain't the blues. A woman with male pattern baldness is. Breaking your leg cuz you skiing is not the blues. Breaking your leg cuz a alligator be chomping on it is.

18. Blues is not a matter of color; it's a matter of bad luck. Tiger Woods cannot sing the Blues. Sonny Liston could have. Ugly white people also got a leg up on the Blues.

19. I don't cares how tragic your life is. If you owns a computer, you can NOT sing the blues. You best destroy it. Blues ways to do this: Fire, a spilled bottle of Mad Dog, or get out a shotgun. Maybe your big woman just done sat on it. I don't care. Jes get rid of it.

What happens if you play blues music backwards?
Your wife returns to you,
Your dog comes back to life,
And you get out of prison.

What does it say on a blues singer's tombstone?
"I didn't wake up this morning..."

CLARKSDALE, MS--Ida Mae Dobbs, longtime woman of Willie "Skipbone" Jackson, called a press conference Tuesday to respond to charges levied against her by the legendary Delta blues singer.

"Despite what Mr. Jackson would have you believe, I am not an evil-hearted woman who will not let him be," Dobbs told reporters. "I repeat: I am not an evil-hearted woman who will not let him be. To the contrary, my lovin' is so sweet, it tastes just like the apple off the tree."

Dobbs, accused of causing Jackson pain and breaking his heart by calling out another man's name, categorically denied treating him in a low-down manner.

"He says he sends for his baby, but I don't come around," Dobbs, a brownskin woman, said. "He says he sends for his baby, but I don't come around. Well, the truth is, I do come, but he is out messing with every gal in town."

During the press conference, Dobbs also disputed an Aug. 27 statement made by Jackson, who compared her to a dresser because someone is always going through her drawers.

"My drawers have not been gone through by any man but Willie "Skipbone" Jackson," Dobbs said. "Neither Slim McGee nor Melvin Brown has ever been in my drawers. Nor has Sonny 'Spoonthumb' Perkins, nor any of those other no-good jokers down by the railroad tracks. My policy has always been to keep my drawers closed to everyone but Mr. Jackson, as I am his woman and would never treat him so unkind."

In addition to denying Jackson's drawer-opening allegations, Dobbs disputed charges of unrestricted sweet-potato-pie distribution, insisting that her pie is available only to Jackson.

"I do not give out my sweet potato pie arbitrarily, as I am not the sort of no-good donkey who engages in such objectionable behavior," Dobbs told reporters. "Only one man can taste my sweet potato pie, and I believe I have made it perfectly clear who that man is." Dobbs noted that the same policy applies to her biscuits, which may be buttered only by Jackson.

While most of the accusations levied against Dobbs relate to her running around town with other men, she does face one far more serious charge, attempted homicide. On May 5, 1998, Jackson was rushed to the hospital and narrowly escaped death after ingesting nearly five ounces of gasoline. Jackson claimed that Dobbs tried to murder him, serving him a glass of the toxic fuel when he requested water. Dobbs dismissed the episode as "an accident."

Dobbs, a short-dress, big-legged woman from Coahoma County, said it is not she but Jackson who should be forced to defend himself. According to Dobbs, Jackson frequently has devilment on his mind, staying up until all hours of the night rolling dice and drinking smokestack lightning.

"Six nights out of seven, he goes off and gets his swerve on while I sit at home by myself. Then he comes knocking on my door at 4 a.m., expecting me to rock him until his back no longer has any bone," Dobbs said. "Is that any way for a man to treat his woman? I don't want to, but if he keeps doing me wrong like this, I am going to take my lovin' and give it to another man."

Added Dobbs: "Skipbone Jackson is going to be the death of me."

Dobbs said that until she receives an apology from Jackson and a full retraction of all accusations, he will not be given any grinding.

"Mr. Jackson says that I stay out all night and that I'm not talking right. He says he has rambling on his mind as a result of my treating him so unkind. He says I want every downtown man I meet and says they shouldn't even let me on the street," Dobbs said. "Well, I refuse to allow my name to be dragged through the mud like this any longer. Unless my man puts an end to these unfair attacks on my character, I will neither rock nor roll him til the break of dawn. I am through with his low-down ways."

42 Classic Justifications
for Stealing Content...

If a music fan is stealing content, it usually comes with a nice, juicy justification. Here are just a few you may have heard...

1. 99 cents is too expensive.
2. I'm broke.
3. This isn't going to the artist, anyway.
4. This pricing doesn't make sense for the way people listen to music.
5. I wouldn't have purchased it anyway, even if I could afford it.
6. Information wants to be free.
7. Music should be for the public, not profit.
8. Labels are dinosaurs. They need to adapt.
9. If I really like the artist, I'll see them on tour. That's where artists make most of their money these days.
10. I just saw the artist on tour.
11. I bought the t-shirt.
12. If I really like the artist, I'll buy the album.
13. I'm not sure if I like this artist.
14. I don't like this artist.
15. This artist is already making bank.
16. This artist totally sold out.
17. It's Nickelback.
18. I've never heard of this artist.
19. It doesn't really hurt the artist.
20. This artist is dead.
21. This artist is almost dead.
22. This artist is greedy.
23. Artists make money off of ads.

24. Artists release their music for free all the time.
25. This money goes to the labels, who don't pay their artists.
26. There's really no difference between downloading something for free and listening to it on Spotify.
27. I buy vinyl all the time.
28. I hate the labels. They're evil and screw artists.
29. Everyone does this.
30. DRM
31. Copyright is rigged for corporations like Disney. It doesn't help music fans.
32. I'm in college.
33. I just graduated college.
34. I'm already paying for Internet access.
35. I ran out of my iTunes allowance.
36. I would pay, but the economy totally sucks.
37. This isn't available on the platform I want to use.
38. This isn't available in the country I live in.
39. I already have this in another format. I shouldn't have to pay twice.
40. I already bought this on another format, and lost it or it was stolen. I shouldn't have to pay twice.
41. When I have more money, I'll pay the artist back.
42. I'm already paying for iTunes Match.

(From Paul, Digital Music News)

Definitely Wanna Hear THIS Set!

"This next song is about my lifelong struggle with tone-deafness and the inability to carry a tune or play an instrument."

"This next one is a hard-rockin', kick-ass, take-no-prisoners tune we wrote about turning sixty."

"This next song is about putting your dreams on hold and doing whatever it takes to pay the rent."

"Here's a song about heartbreak, pain and lost love, which I wrote when I was trying to quit smoking."

"This next song is about the feelings of an expensive, finely crafted instrument spending its life in the hands of a musical hack."

Seventeen Not So Obvious Rules For Ensemble Playing

1. Everyone should play the same piece.
2. Stop at every repeat sign and discuss in detail whether to take the repeat or not. The audience will love this a lot!
3. If you play a wrong note, give a nasty look to one of your partners.
4. Keep your fingering chart handy. You can always catch up with the others.
5. Carefully tune your instrument before playing. That way you can play out of tune all night with a clear conscience.
6. Take your time turning pages.
7. The right note at the wrong time is a wrong note (and vice-versa).
8. If everyone gets lost except you, follow those who get lost.
9. Strive to play the maximum notes per second. That way you gain the admiration of the incompetent.

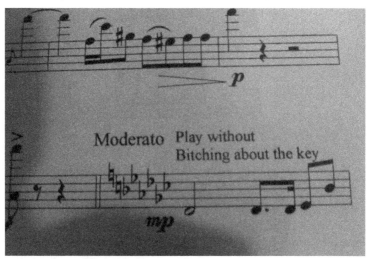

10. Markings for slurs, dynamics and ornaments should not be observed. They are only there to embellish the score.
11. If a passage is difficult, slow down. If it's easy, speed it up. Everything will work itself out in the end.
12. If you are completely lost, stop everyone and say, "I think we should tune."
13. Happy are those who have not perfect pitch, for the kingdom of music is theirs.
14. If the ensemble has to stop because of you, explain in detail why you got lost. Everyone will be very interested.
15. A true interpretation is realized when there remains not one note of the original.
16. When everyone else has finished playing, you should not play any notes you have left.
17. A wrong note played timidly is a wrong note. A wrong note played with authority is an interpretation.

Seventeen Annoying Things You Do And Say That Make Your Band Mates Secretly Hate You

1—"That sounds great, but could you try playing this totally different thing?"

It's not like they spent any time or effort coming up with something special, right? You're just being honest. It totally sounds better your way, right? *RIGHT?!*

2—"We're not playing that set any more. We wrote new songs. Didn't you get the email 2 hours ago?"

Everyone likes new songs, it keeps things fresh! Maybe just a little bit more notice next time, yeah? Maybe a band discussion about it? Possibly?

3—Turning your volume up a tiny bit after every song.

Yeah. We noticed you. Stop that. This is why you're not allowed nice things.

4–Never having cash when it's time to pay for rehearsals.

Every single week? Are you kidding me? No, I don't want all the loose change and fluff from your pockets. *GIVE ME FOLDING MONEY.*

5—Turning up late. To everything. Every. Single. Time.

Do you have some sort of disease that makes it impossible for you turn up on time? We even developed an elaborate system where we tell you a time 2 hours earlier than when we need to arrive. You're *STILL* an hour late.

6—"Do you have a lead / plectrum / stand / strap / guitar I could borrow? I forgot mine."

Once? Fine. Fair enough, everyone's been there. Twice? No biggie, but sort yourself out, yeah? Seventeen times? You do own a lead, right? It's a pretty essential part of being in a band, you know? No, you can't use the one that goes to my effects pedals. Why? Because *GET YOUR OWN LEAD.* That's why.

7—Replacing their takes once they've left the studio.

That's fine. Don't worry. I didn't want to be on this record anyway. It's not like it's been funded with band money I helped make…*OH WAIT, YES IT IS!*

8—Not responding to band communication, then complaining that you don't know what's going on.

Oh, you didn't get the email about this new song? Oh, you got it, *but you just didn't read it?* That's fine, we'll just spend an hour of paid rehearsal time for you to figure it out. Why is that vein popping out of my neck? Oh, no reason. *No reason at all.*

9—Unplugging your equipment when it's still plugged in to a PA at full volume.

Oh, no no, that's fine. I didn't need my hearing, anyway. Maybe you'd like to shove a corkscrew into my ear canal while you're at it? Cheers, mate.

10—Putting your drink anywhere near anyone's equipment.

Yeah, sorry I kicked your pint over, mate. How stupid of me not to see it right beside my effects pedals at the opposite end of the stage to you. My fault entirely...

11—Tuning at full volume.

You know how to turn on the mute mode on your tuner, right? Cool. Ever thought about actually doing it?

12 - Drinking 5 pints before you hit the stage.

Oh, you think you play better when you're "well lubricated", do you? You don't. You're just too drunk to realize you're out of time and playing in the wrong key.

13—Playing while people are trying to communicate in rehearsals.

Don't worry, I love hearing the solo to "Stairway..." when I'm trying to figure out a cool bass line for the song we're actually playing. It's not putting me off at all.

14—Changing parts of songs at the very last minute.

I don't mind sticking a key-change in the last chorus, but to guarantee we all change to *the same key* why not tell us more than 90 seconds before we get on stage? Just a thought.

15—Insulting the sound guy.

So... You turned up late, drunk and with the wrong equipment... but it's the sound guy's fault you sound terrible? Right.

16—Insulting your audience.

"Thanks, you've been a terrible crowd"—*Nice work.* Do you think they would have been a terrible crowd if they'd been watching The Who?... or Bruce Springsteen?... Or any pretty decent local band?

17—Controlling everything. All the time. Always.

Okay, Putin. Is this a rock band or the Soviet Armed Forces? Chillax, mate. I was just seeing if it sounded better on the hat or the ride.

Caveat Emptor!

When starting or surviving while in a band:

- Never start a trio with a married couple.
- Your manager is not helping you, fire him/her.
- Before you sign a record deal, look up the word recoupable in the dictionary.
- No one cares whom you have opened for.
- String sections don't make your song sound any more important.
- If your band has gone through more than four bass players, then it's time to break up.
- When you talk on stage, you're never funny.
- If you sound remarkably like another band, don't act like your unfamiliar with their music.
- Asking a crowd how they are doing is just amplified small talk, don't do it.
- When you get dropped from your record company, insist you had the worst contract ever and you asked to be let go.
- Never name a song after your band.
- Never name your band after a song.
- When the drummer brings in his own songs and asks to perform one of them, begin looking for a new drummer IMMEDIATELY!
- Never enter a battle of the bands contest. If you do, you're already a loser.
- Learn to recognize scary word pairings: "rock opera," "white rapper," "blues jam," "swing band," "open mike," etc…

- Drummers can take off their shirts or wear gloves, but not both.
- Listen, either break it to your parents or we will; it's rock n roll, not a soccer game. They've got to stop coming to your shows.
- It's not a "showcase", it's a gig that doesn't pay.
- No one cares that you've got a website.
- Getting a tattoo is like sewing platform shoes to your feet.
- Don't hire a publicist.
- Playing in San Marcos and Alpine doesn't mean you're on tour.
- Don't join a cover band that plays Bush songs. In fact, don't join a cover band.
- Although they come in different styles and colors, electric guitars all sound the same, why do you keep changing them between songs?
- Don't stop your set to ask that beers be brought up. That's what girlfriends are for.
- If you use a smoke machine, your music sucks.
- We can tell the difference between a professionally produced album and one that you made with the iMac your mom got you for Christmas.
- If blues solos are so difficult, why can so many 16 year olds play them?
- If you ever take a publicity photo, destroy it. You may never know where or when it will turn up.
- Cut your hair, but don't shave your head.
- Pierce your nose, but not your eyebrow.
- Do not wear shorts onstage. Or a suit. Or a hat.
- Rock oxymorons: "major label interest," "demo deal," "blues genius," and the "$500 guarantee."
- Three things that are never coming back: 1.) gongs, 2.) headbands, 3.) playing slide guitar with a beer bottle.

Immediately stop playing and leave the band when:

- Before each gig, you find yourself warming up more parts of your body.
- It becomes more important to find a place onstage for your box fan than your amp.
- During the second set, you scream for the drummer to please stop hitting those annoying cymbals.
- You refuse to play out of tune.
- Your gig clothes look like Donald Trump out for a round of golf.
- Your fans have left by 10:30.
- All you want from groupies is a foot massage.
- You love shopping the dollar store because you can sing along to most of their play list.
- You hire band members for their values instead of their talent.
- You've lost directions to the gig.
- Prepping for the gig involves plucking hair from your chin or nose.
- Most of the hair you've plucked from you chin or nose are gray.
- You need glasses to see your amp settings.
- You've thrown out your back jumping off the stage.
- You're thrilled to have New Year's off.
- The waitress is your daughter = THE BEST!
- You stop the set because your bottle of ibuprofen fell behind the speakers.
- Most of your crowd sways in their seats.
- You find drink tokens from last month's gig in your guitar case.
- You no longer use a tip jar.
- You refuse to play without earplugs.
- You ask the club owner if you can start at 8:30 instead of 9:30.
- You want an opening act.
- You check the TV schedule before booking a gig.

- High notes make you cough.
- Your gig stool has a back.
- You're related to at least one other member of the band.
- You need a nap before the gig.
- You don't let anyone sit in.
- After the third set, you bug the club owner to let you quit early.
- During breaks, you now go to your van to lie down.
- You prefer a music stand with a light.
- You don't recover from a Saturday gig until Tuesday afternoon.
- You can't operate without a set list.
- You say you double on bass.
- You discourage playing longer than contracted.
- You have a contract.
- You hope the host's speech lasts forever.
- You buy amps considering their weight and not their tone or cool factor.
- You feel guilty looking at hot women at the bar because they're younger than your daughter.
- You can remember seven different club names for the same location.
- You have a hazy memory of the days when you could work ten gigs in seven days and could physically do it.
- You think "homey" means cozy and warm.
- You have to look over your glasses to check your PA connections.
- You're playing the same venue in three months and you ask the club owner if you can leave your amp!
- Most of the band members are a lot younger than you.
- Your son is waiting for the gig to end to drive you and your stuff home, then go back out and party.
- Your date couldn't make it because she couldn't find a sitter for the grandkids.
- In consideration of your age, the audience requests some British invasion songs.

- On all out of town gigs you draw straws to see whom the driver will be coming home with.
- You start listing your truss as a "business expense".
- You forget to take your Flowmax so all sets that night are only 15 minutes long.
- When you get a "Cease and Desist" letter from the Spandex Co.
- When you play 2 nights in a row, and the next day your body aches like you played in the Super Bowl!
- When you play a Wednesday night gig and call into work sick on Thursday and Friday.
- When the only "Stones" you care about are in your gallbladder or kidney.
- You have to charge extra money if there are any steps to climb.
- Your hearing has deteriorated so badly that you actually ask the guitar player to "turn himself up."
- You call out the next song only to have someone remind you played it 10 minutes earlier.
- Your drugs are keeping you alive rather than killing you.
- You worry more about breaking a hip than being hip.
- Musicians half your age are in the Rock and Roll Hall of Fame or have appeared on postage stamps.
- The only white powder to be found amongst the band members is foot talc.

NEVER utter the following in a recording session:

- Ready, Freddie (pronounced red-eye fred-eye).
- Bingo, gringo.
- Uno, Bruno.
- The phones sound O.K. but I need more of myself.
- We won't need a click.
- I like what you're trying to do but not the way you're doing it.
- An excellent first attempt.
- Was that the sound you had on the demo?

- Make the click louder.
- That was a pretty good take for this time of night.
- If you want the tempo any brighter than that, we better wait for a sunny day.
- No dynamics? We're playing as loud as we can.
- I think that's a pretty good sounding take for what we're getting paid.
- That was great, let's do it again.
- Is that about as tight as you boys want to get it?
- Is it possible the click is speeding up?
- I'm at the point where I'm making dumb mistakes - before I was making much smarter mistakes.
- So many drummers, so little time.
- Why don't we do the double first. The lead will be easier to get once we've got the double.
- I never had this problem when I was being produced by Jimmy and Terry.
- We got some things, we need some things.
- Fabulous.
- You can't make ice cream out of shit.
- You can't polish a turd.
- Just let your spirit soar.
- My spirit's already sore from the last thirty takes.
- We're getting close.
- Less is more.
- Less is Paul.
- Less is Brown.
- Less is less.
- That's the way I've been playing it all along.
- I just wish I could get a whole band that sounds as good as I do.
- This will be a great opportunity for me to show off my chops.
- Let's hear the bass, if you can call it that.
- Play something Paul would tell Linda to play.
- Does your amp have an under-drive channel?
- You can erase that one, I remember exactly what I played.

- We'll catch that in the mix.
- You guys can fix that in Pro Tools, right?
- I brought my kid along. He's never been in a recording studio before.
- My girlfriend sings great background vocals.
- I know a great drummer.
- You guys want to try some heroin?
- Your girlfriend's been in the bathroom a long time.
- I'm not going to be any more dishonest with you than I am with Donald.
- I'd like a little more of a live feeling on this tune.
- I also play eleven other instruments.
- Sorry I'm late, I just got through with my blood test (or CAT scan).
- That vocal's not a keeper, is it?
- That's how I wrote it but that's not how I like to play it .
- I can't think of any improvements that won't make it worse.
- That ground loop is a trademark thing for me.
- That's the new old comp from today - I want to hear the new old comp from last Tuesday.
- That reverb would sound a lot better if it were coming out of a piece of MY GEAR!
- Skunk called, he's on his way down.
- When was the last time we worked together? Tonight.
- I can see by the clock on the wall that was my best solo—ever!

Begin worrying immediately if you ever hear the following on a musician's tour bus:

- Shouldn't we go back for the drummer?
- Oh, no you don't! It's my turn to clean the bathroom.
- Checkmate!
- Go roll 'em down the aisle all you want. They're only cymbals.
- So, I just walked her home, kissed her goodnight, and came back to the bus.

- No, the monitor mix was perfect. I just screwed up.
- Twenty percent? Our manager should get at least 30 percent!
- Why is there porn in the VCR?
- Can you believe all the money we're getting?
- Boy, I can't wait till we get to Omaha!
- No thanks, I don't want another beer.
- Ladies, I need to see some proof of age please.

NEVER. Produce. A. Record. Like. This.:

First, spend about a month on "preproduction", making sure that everything is completely planned out so that no spontaneity is necessary or possible in the studio. If there are no "hits" there, make the band collaborate with outside songwriters or, better still, cover an old hit. Line up extra studio musicians who are better players than the band themselves, just in case.

Next, book the most expensive studio you can find so that everyone but the band gets paid lots of money. The more expensive, the more the record label will take the project seriously, which is important. Book lots and lots of time. You'll need at least 48 tracks to accommodate all the room mics you'll set up for the drums, all of which will be buried by other instruments later anyway, and for the added keyboard tracks, even if the band has never had a keyboard player. And for all the backing vocal tracks, even if the band only has one singer.

Then, record all the instruments one at a time, but make the drummer play to a click track for every song so the music has no chance to breathe whatsoever. That way you can use lots of MIDI gear. Do multiple takes of each song. Use up at least 30 reels of 2-inch tape. Take the best parts of each take and splice them all together. Because tape and tape machines are so hard to find today, you may want to use a hard-disk recording system like Pro Tools, then transfer it all back to analog two-inch. Spend at least two weeks just compiling drum tracks like this. You'll need to rent at least a half a dozen snare drums, and you'll have to change drumheads every couple of hours. If you really do it right, the entire band will never have to actually play a song together.

Now, start overdubbing each instrument, one at a time. Make sure everything is perfect. If necessary, do things over and over until absolute perfection is achieved. Do a hundred takes if you must. If this doesn't work, get "guest musicians" in to "help out."

Don't forget to hire someone who's good with beats, samples and loops so the kids will think its hip! Better get some turntable scratching on there, too.

Be sure to spend days and days just experimenting with sounds, different amplifiers, guitars, mics, speakers, basically trying every possible option you can think of to use up all that studio time you've booked. No matter how much time you book, you can use it up this way, easily. Everyone involved will think they're working very hard.

Make sure you rent lots of expensive mics and expensive compressors and expensive preamps so you can convince yourself and everyone else how good it's sounding. Charge it to the band's recording budget, of course. Make sure you have at least two or three compressors, in series, on everything you're recording. Any equipment with tubes in it is a sure bet, the older the better. The best is early-1970s-era Neve equipment, old Ampex analog recorders, and WW2-vintage tube microphones, since everyone knows that the technology of recording has continuously declined for the past 30+ years. Don't forget to get some old "ribbon" mics too.

Make sure that by the time it's finished everyone is absolutely, totally sick of all the songs and never wants to hear any of them again. Oops! Now it's time to mix it!

Better get someone with "fresh ears" (who's never heard any of it before) to mix it in a $3000/day SSL room with full automation. Make sure he's pretty famous, and of course you have to fly to LA, NYC or Nashville to do this, because there simply are no decent studios anywhere else. Make sure he compresses the hell out of everything as he mixes it. Compress each drum individually and then compress an overall stereo sub-mix of them. Make sure to compress all the electric guitars even though a distorting guitar amp is the most extreme "compressor" in existence. Compress everything else, and then compress the overall mix. Add tons and tons of reverb to the drums on top of all those room mics, and add stereo chorus on everything else. Spare no expense. Spend at least two weeks on it. Then take it home and decide to pay for someone else to remix the whole thing.

Then get some New York coke-head mastering engineer to master it, and make sure he compresses the hell out of everything again and takes away all the low end and makes it super bright and crispy and harsh so it'll sound really LOUD on the radio. (Too bad about all those people with nice home stereos.)

(Oh-oh! Seems that the A+R guy at the label who loved the project just got fired! Looks like the record will never be released! (Thank goodness!))

There's a good reason why your song didn't get recorded:

- Your song is not pop enough. It never got past the interns at the record company because the interns all like pop and your songs are too country.
- Your song is too pop. The only songs of yours that the interns let through are songs that are not country enough for the producers.
- You sing on your own demos. Have you ever listened to your voice on disc? I mean really listened?

- You think that your little fancy schmancy keyboard has a great string section and you use it on all your home demos.
- The producer put your song on hold too early and was sick of it by the time the session dates came up.
- The producer put your song on hold too late and didn't have time to play it for his artist.
- The artist came off the road with a bunch of songs he had written himself.
- The artist came off the road without having written any songs so they cancelled the session.
- The A&R person didn't like the song.
- The A&R person doesn't like you.
- The A&R person loved the song, but the producer doesn't like the A&R person.
- Your publisher says the producer turned down your song, but he lied. He didn't pitch the song because he doesn't like the song, or he doesn't like you, or he doesn't like the string section on your little fancy schmancy keyboard.
- The producer loved your song enough to find other songs that sound like yours but were written by the artist, or by more successful writers.
- The cd demo of your songs made by your publisher was defective or the mp3s that the publisher sent over sounded terrible.
- Your publisher made a distorted demo version of your music because he hates you.
- The demo is over produced
- The demo is under produced.
- The demo sounds so much like a master that the producer is afraid he won't be able to cut a record that sounds as good.
- The demo singer is so great that the artist is afraid he won't be able to cut a record that sounds as good.
- The producer hates drum machines, or the clavinet, or the lounge organ you added to the demo at the last minute to fill the holes.

- The producer goes ballistic any time he hears a song that rhymes the words "gone" and "alone."
- The A&R person thinks you're and idiot for taking her seriously when she put out the word that she wanted something different this time for her star artist.
- The producer is livid because you have pitched him a wonderful song that sounds like all of his artist's biggest hits—OR he is livid because you have pitched him a wonderful song that doesn't sound anything like his artist's previous hits.
- Your song happened to have been the ninety-eighth song the producer had heard that day. He turned your demo off halfway through the intro.
- The A&R person was furious because her intern had quit the day before, which meant she had to listen to all the tapes on her desk, herself. She didn't like a darn thing she heard all day.
- The A&R person, the producer, and the artist played each other their favorite songs. They argued for a while, and pulled their best power plays. The artist won. You lost. Then they went to dinner together. The record company bought.
- The A&R person loved your song but decided to play it for the secretaries in order to get input from *the people.* The secretaries hated it.
- The label loved your song and made the mistake of playing it for the promotion department. Your song reminded the head of promotion of a song he had written once when he was trying to be a songwriter. He called it a piece of crap and that was the end of your song at *that* label.
- Everybody loved your song until the marketing VP worried that it just wouldn't make a very good video. Then everybody hated it.
- And finally, maybe, just maybe, it's not a very good song. Not a bad song, really, just sort of mediocre. Or, maybe,

as the Emperor of Austria told Mozart, it has, "Too many notes."

- You're just not that good. Neither as a songwriter nor as a singer.

How come kids know this and you don't:
(These are actual stories, test questions, and answers compiled by music teachers in the state of Missouri.)

- Refrain means don't do it. A refrain in music is the part you better not try to sing.
- A virtuoso is a musician with real high morals.
- John Sebastian Bach died from 1750 to the present.
- Handel was half German, half Italian, and half English. He was rather large.
- Beethoven wrote music even though he was deaf. He was so deaf he wrote loud music. He took long walks in the forest even when everyone was calling him. I guess he could not hear so good. Beethoven expired in 1827 and later died from this.
- Henry Purcell is a well-known composer few people have ever heard of.
- Aaron Copland is one of your most famous contemporary composers. It is unusual to be contemporary. Most composers do not live until they are dead.
- An opera is a song of bigly size.
- In the last scene of Pagliacci, Canio stabs Nedda who is the one he really loves. Pretty soon Silvio also gets stabbed, and they all live happily ever after.
- When a singer sings, he stirs up the air and makes it hit any passing eardrums. But if he is good, he knows how to keep it from hurting.
- Music sung by two people at the same time is called a duel.
- I know what a sextet is but I had rather not say.

- Caruso was at first an Italian. Then someone heard his voice and said he would go a long way. And so, he came to America.
- A good orchestra is always ready to play if the conductor steps on the odium.
- Morris dancing is a country survival from times when people were happy.
- Most authorities agree that music of antiquity was written long ago.
- Probably the most marvelous fugue was the one between the Hatfields and McCoys.
- My very best liked piece of music is the Bronze Lullaby.
- My favorite composer is Opus.
- A harp is a nude piano.
- A tuba is much larger than its name.
- Instruments come in many sizes, shapes and orchestras.
- You should always say celli when you mean there are two or more cellos.
- Another name for kettledrums is timpani. But I think I will just stick with the first name and learn it good.
- A trumpet is an instrument when it is not an elephant sound.
- While trombones have tubes, trumpets prefer to wear valves.
- The double bass is also called the bass violin, string bass, and bass fiddle. It has so many names because it is so huge.
- When electric currents go through them, guitars start making sounds. So would anybody.
- Question: What are kettledrums called? Answer: Kettledrums.
- Cymbals are round, metal CLANGS!
- A bassoon looks like nothing I have ever heard.
- Last month I found out how a clarinet works by taking it apart. I both found out and got in trouble.
- Question: Is the saxophone a brass or a woodwind instrument? Answer: Yes.

- The concertmaster of an orchestra is always the person who sits in the first chair of the first violins. This means that when a person is elected concertmaster, he has to hurry up and learn how to play a violin real good.
- For some reason, they always put a treble clef in front of every line of flute music. You just watch.
- I can't reach the brakes on this piano!
- The main trouble with a French horn is it's too tangled up.
- Anyone who can read all the instrument notes at the same time gets to be the conductor.
- Instrumentalist is a many-purposed word for many player-types.
- The flute is a skinny-high shape-sounded instrument.
- The most dangerous part about playing cymbals is near the nose.
- A contra-bassoon is like a bassoon, only more so.
- Tubas are a bit too much.
- Music instrument has a plural known as orchestra.
- I would like for you to teach me to play the cello. Would tomorrow or Friday be best?
- My favorite instrument is the bassoon. It is so hard to play people seldom play it. That is why I like the bassoon best.
- It is easy to teach anyone to play the maracas. Just grip the neck and shake him in rhythm.
- Just about any animal skin can be stretched over a frame to make a pleasant sound once the animal is removed.

Songs Whose Lyrics
Bear A Second Listen

*I'll Bend Over Backwards For You If You'll Bend Over
Frontwards For Me*

I'd Lie To You For Your Love (And That's The Truth)

He Went To Sleep And The Hogs Ate 'Im

*I Hope You're Living As High On The Hog As The Pig You
Turned Out To Be*

If Lovin' You Is Wrong Then I Don't Wanna Be Wrong

Used To Kiss Her On The Lips But Now It's All Over

*How Can I Get Over You If You Don't Get Out From
Underneath Him*

*I Can Spell "Banana" (But I Never Know When To Stop)
(Johnny Mercer)*

If The Phone Doesn't Ring, It's Me (Jimmy Buffett)

If I Were Half The Man You Are, I'd Be Twice The Man I Am

Is It Cold In Here Or Is It Just You

Everyone Has Someone To Love And All I Have Is You

It's So Miserable Without You; It's Almost Like Having You Here

Who Put The Sand In The Vaseline And Hurt The One I Love

Momma, Don't Buy No Fish, 'Cause Daddy's Comin' Home With The Crabs Tonight

Come Back When You Can't Stay So Long

I'm Tryin' To Live Without You, But I Miss Your Unemployment Checks

Show Me The Backdoor, 'Cause My Wife Is Waiting Out Front

Baby, My Heart Is Yours... But The Rest Of Me Is Leavin'

They Say I'm Crazy For You But I Know I'm Just Nuts

Put The Harley In The Shed And Ride On Me Tonight

I Wouldn't Take You to a Dog Fight Even If I Thought You Could Win

My John Deere Was Breaking Your Field, While Your Dear John Was Breaking My Heart"

I Liked You Better Before I Knew You So Well

I Still Miss My Man, But My Aim's Gettin' Better

Her Teeth Was Stained, But Her Heart Was Pure

I Wish I Were in Dixie Tonight, But She's Out of Town

You May Put Me In Prison, But You Can't Keep My Face From Breakin' Out

I Changed Her Oil, She Changed My Life

If My Nose Were Full of Nickels, I'd Blow It All On You

Do You Love As Good As You Look?

Drop Kick Me, Jesus, Through The Goalposts Of Life

Get Your Tongue Outta My Mouth 'Cause I'm Kissing You Goodbye

Here's A Quarter, Call Someone Who Cares

How Can I Miss You If You Won't Go Away?

Been Roped And Thrown By Jesus In The Holy Ghost Corral

I Don't Know Whether To Kill Myself Or Go Bowling

I Fell In A Pile Of You And Got Love All Over Me

I Flushed You From The Toilets Of My Heart

I Keep Forgettin' I Forgot About You

I Wanna Whip Your Cow

I Would Have Wrote You A Letter, But I Couldn't Spell Yuck!

I'd Rather Have A Bottle In Front Of Me Than A Frontal Lobotomy

I'm Just A Bug On The Windshield Of Life

I've Been Flushed From The Bathroom Of Your Heart

If I Can't Be Number One In Your Life, Then Number Two On You

If Love Were Oil, I'd Be A Quart Low

If The Phone Don't Ring, Baby, You'll Know It's Me

If You Don't Leave Me Alone, I'll Go And Find Someone Else Who Will

If You Leave Me, Can I Come Too

Mama Get The Hammer (There's A Fly On Papa's Head)

May The Bird Of Paradise Fly Up Your Nose

My Every Day Silver Is Plastic

My Wife Ran Off With My Best Friend, And I Sure Do Miss Him

Oh, I've Got Hair Oil On My Ears And My Glasses Are Slippin' Down, But Baby I Can See Right Through You

Pardon Me, I've Got Someone To Kill

She Got The Gold Mine And I Got The Shaft

She Got The Ring And I Got The Finger

She Made Toothpicks Out Of The Timber Of My Heart

She's Got Freckles On Her, But She's Pretty

Thank God And Greyhound She's Gone

Velcro Arms, Teflon Heart.

When You Leave, Walk Out Backwards, So I'll Think You're Walking In

You Can't Have Your Kate And Edith Too

You Can't Roller Skate In A Buffalo Herd

You Done Tore Out My Heart And Stomped That Sucker Flat

You Were Only A Splinter In My Ass As I Slid Down The Bannister Of Life

You're The Reason Our Kids Are So Ugly

Special Feature! Jewish Country-Western Songs

I Was One of the Chosen People ('Til She Chose Somebody Else)

Honky Tonk Nights on the Golan Heights

I've Got My Foot on the Glass, Where Are You

My Rowdy Friend Elijah's Coming Over Tonight

New Bottle of Whiskey, Same Old Testament

Stand by Your Mensch

Eighteen Wheels and a Dozen Latkes

I Balanced Your Books, but You're Breakin' My Heart

My Darlin's a Schmendrick and I'm All Verklempt

That Shiksa Done Made off With My Heart Like a Goniff

The Second Time She Said 'Shalom,' I Knew It Meant Goodbye

You're the Lox My Bagel's Been Missin'

You've Been Talkin' Hebrew in Your Sleep Since that Rabbi Came to Town

Mamas Don't Let Your Ungrateful Sons Grow Up to Be Cowboys
(When They Could Very Easily Have Just Taken Over the Family Hardware Business that My Own Grandfather Broke His Back to Start and My Father Built Up Over Years of Effort Which Apparently Doesn't Mean Anything Now That You're Turning Your Back on Such a Gift!)

And for the best of the best:

Whether you are a country music fan or not, these are the words of a deep thinker and highly intelligent person. Simple, yet so profound! These are words of wisdom from a famous philosopher, iconic country music singer, on the occasion of his 75th birthday. Only a man with such wisdom and maturity could be so concise and succinct in phrasing his feelings at this turning point in his life.

"I Have Outlived My Pecker"
By Willie Nelson

My nookie days are over,
my pilot light is out.
What used to be my sex appeal,
is now my water spout.
Time was when, on its own accord,
from my trousers, it would spring.
But now I've got a full-time job,
to find the f*** in' thing.

It used to be embarrassing,
the way it would behave.
For every single morning,
it would stand and watch me shave.
Now as old age approaches,
it sure gives me the blues.
To see it hang its little head,
and watch me tie my shoes!

"O.K., this time with a little less feeling."

Heavenly Sounds

Donald Trump arrived at the Pearly Gates this week, and was met by St. Peter. Trump was stunned for a moment.

"You mean, I---I'm in?" he asked.

"That's right" said St. Peter. "Come on, man. I'll show you around." He tossed the keys to a brand-new Ferrari at Trump, and said, "You drive. This is your car, for the rest of eternity."

Trump was buoyant as they drove along the streets of Heaven, through sunny neighborhoods. Finally, they came to a fancy part of town, with big lawns and swimming pools. St. Peter told Trump that this is where he would be living.

"That's Franklin Roosevelt's house over there," St. Peter pointed out as they drove, "And that's where Albert Einstein lives, next to Madame Curie. Pope John Paul XXIII lives here. And, here's your house." They pulled into the driveway, and got out.

As Trump was looking around, he noticed up in the hills a palace made of shimmering, white granite. He could see it was enormous, with room after room, and terraces with dozens of gold fountains. "That must be where the Lord lives," said Trump. St. Peter shook his head.

"No, that's Ray Charles' place," he said. Trump's smile faltered for a moment.

"Ray Charles lives there? How come all the presidents, scientists and popes live here, and Ray Charles lives up in that palace? I don't get it."

St. Peter chuckled. "Donnie," he said, "Presidents and Popes are a dime a dozen. But baby, there's only one Ray Charles."

A guitarist dies and is quite pleased to find that he ends up standing before the pearly gates of Guitar Heaven. St. Peter shows him in, and gives him a guided tour.

"This is Stevie Ray's room here...," says Peter, and the guitarist is saying, "Wow! Stevie Ray!"

"And, this is Jimi's room..." and the guitarist is totally over the moon.

Finally, Peter shows the guitarist to his own room. Before Peter leaves, he says to him, "I have to ask. Is Yngwie here?" Peter shakes his head sadly and says, "I'm afraid he went... the "other" way..."

The guitarist is disappointed but goes to his room and tries to get some sleep. He is woken up in the middle of the night by someone playing a really fast harmonic minor lick - and it sounds just like Yngwie. He presses his ear to the wall, and listens more closely. Someone in the next room is playing really fast neo-classical shreds through what sounds very much like a vintage Strat.

The guitarist is confused as it sounds so much like Yngwie. The next day he tells Peter that he is almost certain that Yngwie's in the next room.

Peter pulls him to one side, and whispers into his ear, "Shhh.... don't tell anyone. That's God. He thinks he's Yngwie Malmsteen."

Saint Peter is checking in new arrivals in heaven....

Arrival 1. "What did you do on Earth?" "I was a surgeon. I helped the lame to walk." "Well, go right on in through the Pearly Gates."

Arrival 2. "What did you do on Earth?" "I was a school teacher. I taught the blind to see." "Fine. Go right on in through the Pearly Gates!"

Arrival 3. "What did you do on Earth?" "I was a musician. I helped make sad people happy." "You can load in through the kitchen."

The organ is the instrument of worship for in its sounding we sense the Majesty of God and in its ending, we know the Grace of God.

A jazz pianist dies and finds himself in heaven. He runs into an old friend and says, "Bob, you made it too, that's great." "Yeah, it turns out God's a big jazz fan. All of the cats are here, and every day is a non-stop jam session with a never-ending supply of wine, women and food. There's just one drawback." "What's that?"

"Well, God has a girlfriend, and she's a singer."

A sax player dies and goes to the pearly gates. St Peter says, "Sorry, too much partying - you have to go to the other place." He takes the elevator down. The elevator doors open and he goes into a huge bar. All the greatest are on stage, on a break. He goes over to Charlie Parker and says, "Hey this can't be Hell, all the best cats are playing here. Parker say's, "Hey man, Karen Carpenter is on drums!"

A bass player dies and immediately finds himself in the afterlife. He looks around to see that he's in a recording studio, holding his bass. Behind him, the drummer is Jeff Porcaro. On his left, Jimi Hendrix is tuning his guitar. Looking around, the bass player notices Marvin Gaye in the vocal booth. "Wow," he thinks, "This must be Heaven!" Then the talkback comes on and an unearthly voice says, "OK, from the top: *Tie a Yellow Ribbon*, take 1,139."

There was this dumb soprano who had just died. When she got to the Pearly Gates, St. Peter says, "You can get into Heaven if you answer this question: What is the name of God's Son?" The soprano says, "Let me think about it." So she did. She returns to the Pearly Gates and says, "I've got it!" "OK, shoot," he says. "It's Andy!" Andy? "Yeah, Andy! You know, Andy walks with me and talks with me?"

What's the difference between God and a conductor?
God knows He's not a conductor.

A musician arrived at the pearly gates. "What did you do when you were alive?" asked St. Peter. "I was the principal trombone player of the London Symphony Orchestra." "Excellent! We have a vacancy in our celestial symphony orchestra for a trombonist. Why don't you turn up at the next rehearsal?" So, when the time for the next rehearsal arrived, our friend turned up with his heavenly trombone [*sic*]. As he took his seat God moved, in a mysterious way, to the podium and tapped his baton to bring the players to attention. Our friend turned to the angelic second trombonist (!) and whispered, "So, what's God like as a conductor?" "Oh, he's O.K. most of the time, but occasionally he thinks he's Von Karajan."

Saint Peter is checking ID's at the Pearly Gates, and first comes a Texan. "Tell me, what have you done in life?" says St. Peter.

The Texan says, "Well, I struck oil, so I became rich, but I didn't sit on my laurels--I divided all my money among my entire family in my will, so our descendants are all set for about three generations."

St. Peter says, "That's quite something. Come on in. Next!"

The second guy in line has been listening, so he says, "I struck it big in the stock market, but I didn't selfishly just provide for my own like that Texan guy. I donated five million to Save the Children."

"Wonderful!" says Saint Peter. "Come in. Who's next?"

The third guy has been listening, and says timidly with a downcast look, "Well, I only made five thousand dollars in my entire lifetime."

"Heavens!" says St. Peter. "What instrument did you play?"

When asked by the Pope (I forget which one) what the Catholic Church could do for music, Igor Stravinsky is reputed to have answered without hesitation: "Give us back *castrati*!"

Noah Forms A Band

And so, in the dark of night the Lord awoke Noah, and spoke to him. "Noah, awake and heed my words!"

And Noah, being afraid and disoriented, did cry out, "Who goeth there?"

And the Lord did smite him upside the head, saying, "It is the Lord of all things, dummy!"

And Noah did tremble, saying, "Lord, why hast Thou wakened me?" And the Lord did say, "Noah, build me a Jobbing Band. For the earth will be visited by a plague of Brides, followed by forty days of Trade Shows and forty nights of Awards Banquets." And Noah did say, "But Lord, will I not be thy Leader?'

And the Lord did smite him again, saying, "Fool, thou wilt be my Contractor. Ask not why!" And Noah did bow his head, saying, "Yes, my Lord. And what will this Leader play?" And the Lord said, "It mattereth little, whether he play or not, or whether he be proficient or not. For his job shall primarily be to talk to the Brides and their Mothers, and to deal with Clients, and to count off Tempos wrong, and to inquire as to whether Overtime will happen, and to try to segue tunes that should not be segued. If he playeth any instrument, thou must always have another player of that instrument in the band, just to be safe."

And Noah did say, "And what else shall this Leader do?" And the Lord replied, "It shall be his job to spread Bad Information and Confusion amongst the Sidemen, and to pit them one against the other, and to delay all Payments." "Further shall it be his job, until we can afford a Soundman, to create Feedback, and to invent new Equalization Curves therefore." And Noah did shake his head in wonder, saying, "Lord, thy ways are Strange and Mysterious. What more shall I do?"

And the Lord said, "Next, find Me a Rhythm Section. "First, find me a Drummer. And three things above all must this Drummer possess." And Noah did ask, "What are these three things? Double Bass Drums? An Electronic Kit? Congas?" And the Lord did smite Noah again, saying, "Second-guess Me not, my servant. First, this Drummer must have slightly imperfect time, so that whenever he playeth a Fill (and he shall play many), he always emergeth at a different place, sometimes early and sometimes late, but thou may not guess which. And second, he must be Supremely Discontent, always hoping for the Big Break which will lead to him playing with Chick Corea or Madonna, so that he despiseth Jobbing. And third, he must always be convinced of his Righteousness in all things, including Time, Volume, Tempo and Feel, so that he argueth always with the Bass Player."

And Noah did say, "As you command, Lord. And what next?" And the Lord did say, "Thou art learning, Noah. Next shall be the Bass Player. And he shall be Bored. That is all."

And Noah did say, "Of course. And next, my Lord?" "Next shall be the Keyboard Player. And he shall play as if he has twenty fingers, and he shall play Substitute upon Substitute, until no man may name the Chord, and he will not be helpful. Furthermore, he shall always be Late. And, he shall always be trying out New Gear, of which he has no knowledge."

And Noah did wonder aloud, "Lord, great is Thy Wisdom!" "Next shall be the Guitar Player. And he shall be a Rock Guitar Player. And he shall be Loud, and he shall sing 'Old Time Rock n' Roll'. Also, shall he not know The Page, and so shall rely upon his Ears, which have been damaged by exposure to High Sound Pressure Levels. For the Guitarists who Read, shall already be playing Shows, and will be making the Big Shekels. And his tux shall be the Rattiest." And Noah did say, "It shall be done."

And the Lord did say, "Next, thou shall need Horns. First shall be the Saxophones. And ye shall know them as Beboppers. And they shall play their Bird Quotes in every song, yea, even the Celine Dion ballad. And they shall Get High on every break, and make the Long Faces all night long, but especially when 'In The Mood' is called."

"Next, shall be the Trumpeters. And they shall, every one, attempt to take everything Up an Octave, and fail frequently. And of Changes they shall know nothing."

"And finally, shall be the Trombone Player. And many jokes will be made about him, for he will have a Beeper, as well as a Day Job, and he will be the first to be Cut from the Band."

And Noah, taking many notes, did say, "Mighty is the Lord!" "Next shall be the String Players. Find me Three Women, and attach pickups to their Violins that are more ancient even than Myself, so that their instruments screecheth and causeth great pain. And their job shall be to dress in Evening Gowns, and to Fake Parts on all Ballads, and to occasionally Stroll, and to complain about the Volume, and the Intonation, and to impede the Swing."

And Noah did say, "What else can be left, Lord?" And the Lord did say, "Finally, find me the Singers. And they shall be three, one a Male, and two Females. And the Male shall be a Strutting Peacock, with the Rock 'n Roll Hair, and he shall never have to wear The Tuxedo, and also shall he play The Harmonica. And of the Females, one shall be Black and one shall be White. And the Black one shall ALWAYS sing the Aretha songs, and the Disco. And the White one shall ALWAYS sing the Power Ballads, and the Country Songs. But both shall share the Motown Medley, and shall sing Backup for the Male, and forget the Words, and be Late, and know nothing of Keys or Form. And they shall leave every gig immediately, having never touched a piece of Equipment. And they shall be paid many more shekels than the Sidemen. Ask not why." And Noah did say, "As Thou sayest, my Lord."

And the Lord did command him, "Search high and low for these, as not every musician can fulfill these requirements. And though we have No Work yet, a Commitment must be secured from All. And while you're at it, start looking for Subs." And Noah did say, "Lord, Thy will be done." And it was.

Let There Be Bass

In the beginning, there was a bass. It was a Fender, probably a Precision, but it could have been a Jazz - nobody knows. Anyway, it was very old ... definitely pre-C.B.S.

And God looked down upon it and saw that it was good. He saw that it was very good in fact, and couldn't be improved on at all (though men would later try.) And so, He let it be and He created a man to play the bass.

And lo the man looked upon the bass, which was a beautiful 'sunburst', and he loved it. He played upon the open E string and the note rang through the earth and reverberated throughout the firmaments (thus reverb came to be.) And it was good. And God heard that it was good and He smiled at his handiwork.

Then in the course of time, the man came to slap upon the bass. And lo it was funky.

And God heard this funkiness and He said, "Go man, go." And it was good.

And more time passed, and, having little else to do, the man came to practice upon the bass. And lo, the man came to have upon him a great set of chops. And he did play faster and faster until the notes rippled like a breeze through the heavens.

And God heard this sound, which sounded something like the wind, which He had created earlier. It also sounded something like the movement of furniture, which He hadn't even created yet, and He was not so pleased. And He spoke to the man, saying, "Don't do that!"

Now the man heard the voice of God, but he was so excited about his new ability that he slapped upon the bass a blizzard of funky notes. And the heavens shook with the sound, and the Angels ran about in confusion. (Some of the Angels started to dance, but that's another story.)

And God heard this - how could He miss it - and lo He became Bugged. And He spoke to the man, and He said, "Listen man, if I wanted Jimi Hendrix I would have created the guitar. Stick to the bass parts."

And the man heard the voice of God, and he knew not to mess with it. But now he had upon him a passion for playing fast and high. The man took the frets off of the bass that God had created. And the man did slide his fingers upon the fretless fingerboard and play melodies high upon the neck. And, in his excitement, the man did forget the commandment of the Lord, and he played a frenzy of high melodies and blindingly fast licks. And the heavens rocked with the assault and the earth shook, rattled and rolled.

Now God's wrath was great. And His voice was thunder as He spoke to the man.

And He said, "O.K. for you, pal. You have not heeded My word. Lo, I shall create a soprano saxophone and it shall play higher than you can even think of."

"And from out of the chaos I shall bring forth the drums. And they shall play so many notes thine head shall ache, and I shall make you to always stand next to the drummer."

"You think you're loud? I shall create a stack of Marshall guitar amps to make thine ears bleed. And I shall send down upon the earth other instruments, and lo, they shall all be able to play higher and faster than the bass."

"And for all the days of man, your curse shall be this; that all the other musicians shall look to you, the bass player, for the low notes. And if you play too high or fast all the other musicians shall say "Wow" but really, they shall hate it. And they shall tell you you're ready for your solo career, and find other bass players for their bands. And for all your days if you want to play your fancy licks you shall have to sneak them in like a thief in the night."

"And if you finally do get to play a solo, everyone shall leave the bandstand and go to the bar for a drink."

And it was so.

23rd Psalm For Bassists and Drummers....

The Lord is my drummer, I shall not rush.
He maketh me to lay out in tasteful places.
He leadeth me beside cool meter changes.
He restoreth the "one".
Yea though I read through the trickiest charts,
I will fear no evil.

For You are with it.
Your ride and Your snare, they comfort me.
Thou prepareth a solo before me
In the presence of mine guitarists.
Thou annointeth my lines with soul.
My groove runneth over.

Surely, goodness and music will come from me,
all the days of my life.
And, I will dwell in the pocket for ever and ever.

I See The Light!

How many producers does it take to change a light bulb?
Hmm...I don't know...what do *you* think?

How many IATSE members does it take to change a light bulb?
Eight... you got a problem with that!?!

How many soundmen does it take to change a light bulb?
"One, two, three, one, two, three..."
"Hey man, I just do sound."
One. Upon finding no replacement, he takes the original apart, repairs it with a chewing gum wrapper and duct tape, changes the screw mount to bayonet mount, finds an appropriate patch cable, and re-installs the bulb fifty feet from where it should have been, to the satisfaction of the rest of the band.

How many Deadheads does it take to change a light bulb?

12,001. One to change it, 2,000 to record the event and take pictures of it, and 10,000 to follow it around until it burns out.

How many jazz musicians does it take to change a light bulb?

None. Jazz musicians can't afford light bulbs.

"Don't worry about the changes. We'll fake it!"

How many punk-rock musicians does it take to change a light bulb?

Two: One to screw in the bulb and the other to smash the old one on his forehead.

How many folk musicians does it take to change a light bulb?

Five. One to change the bulb and four others to complain that it's electric.

How many country & western singers does it take to change a light bulb?

Three. One to change the bulb and two to sing about the old one.

How many 2nd violinists does it take to change a light bulb?

None, they can't get up that high.

How many bass players does it take to change a light bulb?

1. None. The piano player can do that with his left hand.
2. Don't bother. Just leave it out. No one will notice.
3. One. But, the guitarist has to show him first.
4. One. Five. One. Five...
5. Six. One to change it and the other five to fight off the lead guitarists who are hogging the light.
6. 1...5...1... (1...4...5...5...1)
7. None. They're so macho they prefer to walk in the dark and bang their shins.

How many clarinetists does it take to change a light bulb?

Only one, but he'll go through a whole box of bulbs before he finds just the right one.

How many trumpet players does it take to change a light bulb?

Five. One to handle the bulb and four to tell him how much better they could have done it.

How many French horn players does it take to change a light bulb?

Just one, but he'll spend two hours checking the bulb for alignment and leaks.

How many tuba players does it take to change a light bulb?

Three. One to hold the bulb and two to drink 'till the room spins.

How many drummers does it take to change a light bulb?

"Why? Oh, wow! Is it like dark, man?"

Only one, but he'll break ten bulbs before figuring out that they can't just be pushed in.

Two: one to hold the bulb, and one to turn his throne (but only after they figure out that you have to turn the bulb).

Twenty. One to hold the bulb, and nineteen to drink until the room spins.

None. They have a machine to do that.

How many lead guitarists does it take to change a light bulb?

1. None. They just steal somebody else's light.
2. At least 2,000. One to change the bulb and 1999 to insist how much better they could've done it!

How many vocalists does it take to change a light bulb?

One. She holds the bulb and the world revolves around her.

Two. One to hold the diet cola and the other to get her accompanist to do it.

Four. One to change the bulb and three to pull the chair out from under her.

How many alto saxes does it take to screw in a light bulb?

None. They can't get that high.

Two. One to screw it in and the other to say, "Isn't that a little high for you?"

Five. One to change the bulb and four to contemplate how David Sanborn would have done it.

How many tenor saxes does it take to change a light bulb?

Four. One to change the bulb and three to bitch that they could have done it if they had the high notes.

How many trombonists does it take to change a light bulb?

Just one, but he'll do it too loudly.

How many mosquitoes does it take to screw in a light bulb?

Two, but don't ask how they got in the light bulb in the first place.

(We know it's not a musician joke, but we liked it anyway)

In the 22th century, how many guitar players will you need to replace a light source?

Five. One to actually do it, and four to reminisce about how much better the old tubes were.

The Ten Commandments of Rock & Roll

I—Always suck up to the Top Cats.

II—Do not express independent opinions.

III—Make devastating judgments on persons and situations without adequate information.

IV—If there's nothing to complain about, dig up some old gripe.

V—Do not respect property or persons other than band property or personnel.

VI—Do not work for common interest, only your own interest.

VII—Discourage and confound personal, technical and/or creative projects.

VIII—Single out absent persons for intense criticism.

IX—Remember that anything you don't understand is trying to fuck with you.

X—Destroy yourself physically and morally and insist that all true brothers do likewise as an expression of unity.

I want(ed) one!

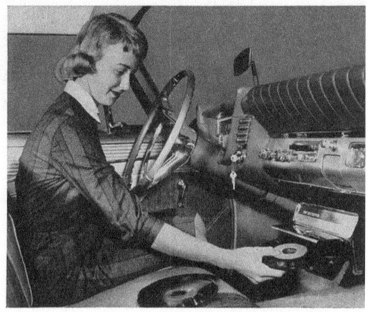

This RCA automatic record player provides motorists with up to two hours of continuous entertainment from 45-rpm records. Available as an accessory in 1960 Plymouth and DeSoto cars, it is the first automobile type to use readily available standard phonograph records.

MUSIC –

The other non-addictive, mood altering non-substance.

Ask your Doctor if music is right for you.

Common side effects include but are not limited to:
Uncontrolled head bobbing
Toe tapping
Finger snapping
Selective hearing impairment
Persistent melody flashbacks

New Gear On The Block

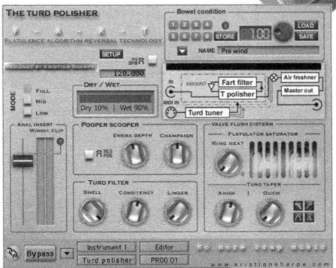

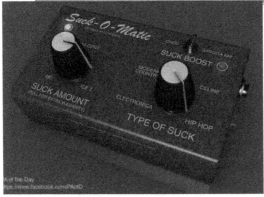

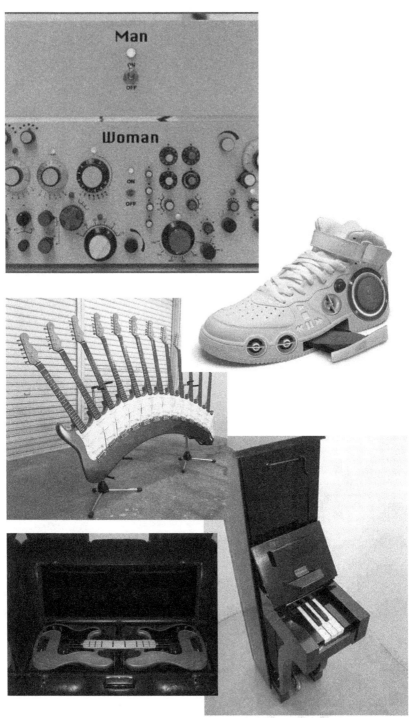

Piano for Rap

Glossary of Terms

A 440: The highway that runs around Nashville.

Accent: An unnatural manner of pronunciation, eg: "Ya'll sang that real good!"

Accidentals: Wrong notes.

Ad Libitum: A premiere.

Agent: A character who resents performers getting 90% of his salary.

Agitato: A string player's state of mind when a peg slips in the middle of a piece.

Allegro: Leg fertilizer.

Altos: Not to be confused with "Tom's toes," "Bubba's toes" or "Dori-toes."

Angus Dei: A woman composer famous for her church music.

Arpeggio: "Ain't he that storybook kid with the big nose that grows?"

Arranger: A guy who writes to support a drinking habit.

Attica: "Fire at will!"

Audition: The act of putting oneself under extreme duress to satisfy the sadistic intentions of someone who has already made up his mind.

Augmented Fifth: A 36-ounce bottle.

Bach Chorale: The place behind the barn where you keep the horses.

Ballet: An art form for people with eating disorders.

Bandstand: The area furthest away from an electrical outlet.

Bar Line: a gathering of people, usually among which may be found a musician or two.

Bass: The things you run around in softball.

Bass Clef: Where you wind up if you fall off (See Clef).

Bassoon: 1. Typical response when asked what you hope to catch, and when. 2. A bedpost with a bad case of gas.

Beat: What music students do to each other with their musical instruments. The downbeat is performed on the top of the head, while the up-beat is struck under the chin.

Big Band: Nowadays, an aggregation consisting of two musicians.

Bossa Nova: The car your foreman drives.

Bravo: Literally, "How bold!" or "What nerve!" This is a spontaneous expression of appreciation on the part of the concert goer after a particularly trying performance.

Breve: The way a sustained note sounds when a violinist runs out of bow.

Broadway Pit Job: A prison sentence disguised as a gig.

Broken Consort: When someone in the ensemble has to leave to go to the bathroom.

Cabaret: a venue where singers do songs from shows that closed out of town.

Cadence: 1. The short nickname of a rock group whose full name is Cadence Clearwater Revival. 2. When everybody hopes you're going to stop, but you don't (Final Cadence: when they FORCE you to stop.).

Cadenza: 1. That ugly thing your wife always vacuums dog hair off of when company comes. 2. The heroine in Monteverdi's opera Frottola.

Cantus Firmus: The part you get when you can only play four notes.

Carpal Tunnel Syndrome: God's way of telling you that you've practiced too much.

Caterer: A man whose hatred for musicians is unrivaled.

Cello: The proper way to answer the phone.

Chansons De Geste: Dirty songs.

Chanteuse: A singer with an accent and no time.

Chord: Usually spelled with an "s" on the end, means a particular type of pants, eg: "He wears chords."

Chromatic Scale: An instrument for weighing that indicates half-pounds.

Clarinet: Name used for your second daughter if you've already used Betty Jo.

Classical Composer: A man ahead of his time and behind in the rent.

Clausula: Mrs. Santa Claus.

Clef: 1. If a student cannot sing, he may have an affliction of the palate, called a clef. 2. Something to jump from if you can't sing and you have to teach elementary school. 3. Something not to fall off of.

Clubdater: God's way of telling you that you didn't practice enough.

Club Date Leader: Someone who changes his name from Kaminsky to Kaye.

Coloratura Soprano: A singer who has great trouble finding the proper note, but who has a wild time hunting for it.

Compound Meter: A place to park your car that requires two dimes.

Conduct: The type of air vents in a prison, especially designed to prevent escape. Could also be installed for effective use in a practice room.

Conductor: 1. A musician who is adept at following many people at the same time. 2. The man who punches your ticket to Birmingham.

Continental Violinist: A guy who rushes like he's trying to catch the last train to Budapest.

Contractor: A man whose funeral nobody goes to.

Counterpoint: 1. A favorite device of many Baroque composers, all of whom are dead, though no direct connection between these two facts has been established. Still taught in many schools, as a form of punishment. 2. Two guitarists sight-reading the same line.

Countertenor: A singing waiter.

Crescendo: A reminder to the performer that he has been playing too loudly.

Cruise Ship Work: A gig that gives a musician two reasons to throw up.

Crying Shame: There was an empty seat.

Cut Time: 1. Parole. 2. When you're going twice as fast as everyone else in the orchestra.

Cymbal: What they use on deer-crossing signs so you know what to sight-in your pistol with.

Detache: An indication that the trombones are to play with the slides removed.

Diatonic: Low-calorie Schweppes (see Tonic).

Di Lasso: Popular with Italian cowboys.

Diminished Fifth: An empty bottle of Jack Daniels (See Perfect Fifth).

Dischord: Not to be confused with Datcord.

DJ: The guy your son would rather have play his Bar Mitzvah.

Dominant: An adjective used to describe the voice of a child who sings off key.

Doublebass: The instrument the folks footing the bill feel is unnecessary.

Downbeat: The magazine that would have you believe that all jazz musicians are working.

Ducita: A lot of mallards.

Duple Meter: May take an even number of coins (see Triple Meter).

Duration: Can be used to describe how long a music teacher can exercise self-control.

Electric Piano: The instrument that enables its player to pay for the hernia he sustained lifting it.

English Horn: Neither English nor a horn. Not to be confused with the French horn, which is German.

Espressivo: Close eyes and play with a wide vibrato.

Estampie: What they put on letters in Quebec.

Fermata: A brand of girdle made especially for opera singers.

First Inversion: Grandpa's battle group at Normandy.

Flat: This is what happens to a tonic if it sits too long in the open air.

Flue: A sophisticated peashooter with a range of up to 500 yards, blown transversely to confuse the enemy.

Form: 1. The shape of a composition. 2. The shape of the musician playing the composition. 3. The piece of paper to be filled out in triplicate in order to get enough money from the Arts Council to play the composition.

French horn: Your wife says you smell like a cheap one when you come in at 4 a.m.

Glissando: 1. The musical equivalent of slipping on a banana peel. 2. A technique adopted by string players for difficult runs.

Half Step: 1. The pace used by a cellist when carrying his instrument. 2. Two oboes playing in unison.

Harmonic Minor: A good music student.

Harmony: A corn-like food eaten by people with accents (see above for definition of accent).

Hemiola: A hereditary blood disease caused by chromatics.

Heroic Tenor: A singer who gets by on sheer nerve and tight clothing.

Hotel Pianist: A guy who looks good in a tux.

Interval: The amount of time it takes to find the right note. There are three kinds: 1. Major interval: a long time. 2. Minor interval: a few bars. 3. Inverted interval: when you have to go back a bar and try again.

Intonation: Singing through one's nose. Considered highly desirable in the Middle Ages.

Isorhythmic Motet: When half of the ensemble got a different edition from the other half.

Jazz: The only true American art form beloved by Europeans.

Jazz Festival: An event attended by folks who think Coltrane is a car on the B&O railroad.

Lamentoso: With handkerchiefs.

Lucky Break: When a busload of bass players goes off a cliff.

Lyric: That part of a tune known only by singers.

Major Scale: What you say after chasing wild game up a mountain: "Damn! That was a major scale!"

Major Triad: The name of the head of the Music Department. (Minor Triad: The name of the wife of the head of the Music Department.)

Mean-Tone Temperament: One's state of mind when everybody's trying to tune at the same time.

Mellophone: An instrument best put to use when converted into a lamp.

Meter Signature: The name of the maid who writes you a ticket when you put an odd number of coins in a duple meter.

Metronome: 1. A city-dwelling dwarf. 2. The archenemy of chanteuses and cantors.

Middle C: The only fruit drink you can afford when food stamps are low.

Minnesinger: A boy soprano.

Minor Second: Two oboists playing in perfect unison.

Minor Third: Your approximate age and grade at the completion of formal schooling.

Modulation: "Nothing is bad in modulation."

Movie Composer: Someone who can write like anyone except himself.

Music: A complex organization of sounds, akin to noise and cacophony, which is set down by the composer, incorrectly interpreted by the conductor, who is ignored by the musicians, the result of which is ignored by the audience.

Musica Ficta: When you lose your place, and have to bluff until you find it again.

Nerd: Someone who owns his own alto clarinet.

New Age: A musical substitute for Valium.

New Year's Eve: The night of the year when contractors are forced to hire musicians they despise.

Notes: Small, folded pieces of paper passed by students during music class.

Oboe: An ill wind that nobody blows good.

Orchestrator: The musician who enhances a composer's music, only to be chastised for it.

Order of Sharps: What a wimp gets at the bar.

Parallel Minor: A music student who is as tall as his instructor.

Passing Tone: Frequently heard near the baked beans at family barbecues.

Percussionist: A drummer who can't swing.

Perfect Fifth: A full bottle of Jack Daniels.

Perfect Pitch: 1. The ability to toss a clarinet into a toilet without hitting the rim. 2. The smooth coating on a freshly paved road. 3. The ability to pinpoint any note and still play out of tune.

Phrase: What teaching music does to your nerves.

Pianissimo: "Refill this beer bottle."

Pianist: An archaic term for a keyboard player.

Piano Subito: Indicates an opportunity for some obscure orchestra player to become a soloist.

Pitch: A tossing motion frequently used by orchestral players to hand in music.

Piu: A descriptive slang term.

Pizzicato: A small Italian pie garnished with cheese, anchovies, etc.

Plague: A collective noun, as in "a plague of conductors."

Portamento: A foreign country you've always wanted to see.

Prepatory Beat: A threat made to singers, eg: "Sing or else!"

Prima Donna: The soprano who generally dies in the last act of an opera of consumption (or frequently, of over-consumption).

Prodigy: A kid who has as much chance at a normal childhood as the Chicago Cubs winning the World Series, again.

Quarter tone: 1. A harpist tuning unison strings. 2. What most standard pickups can haul.

Quaver: Beginning violinists. (Semi-Quaver: Intermediate violinists)

Raga: The official music of New York's Taxi and Limousine Commission.

Rare Violin: A Stradivarius, not to be confused with a rare violinist, which is someone over four foot eleven.

Refrain: Don't do it. A refrain is the part of music you'd better not sing.

Relative Major: An uncle in the Marine Corps.

Relative Minor: A guitarist's girlfriend.

Repeat: What you do until they just expel you.

Resolution: An oath frequently made by music teachers, eg: "I'll never use that song again!"

Rhythm: A term found frequently in religious songs, eg: "He has rhythm from the dead!"

Risoluto: Indicates to the orchestra that they are to stubbornly maintain the correct tempo no matter what the conductor tries to do.

Ritard: There's one in every family.

Rubato: German measles.

Sensible: This term is occasionally seen in Italian opera scores, but it obviously is a misnomer.

Senza Sordino: A term used to remind the string player that he forgot to put his mute on a few measures back.

Sequence: Small, faceted ornaments sewn to a performer's costume which sparkle in the lights.

Sharp: An adjective used to describe another musician whose opinions are in harmony with your own.

Sideman: The appellation that guarantees a musician will never be rich.

Slur: As opposed to madam.

Sonata: What you get from a bad cold or hay fever.

Soprano Sofege: do, re, mi, me, ME, Not You, ME!!

Staccato: How you did all the ceilings in your mobile home.

Staff Musician: Harder to locate than a cavity in the Osmond family.

Steady Engagement: Look up the definition of "obsolete."

String Quartet: A good violinist, a bad violinist, an ex-violinist, and someone who hates violinists, all getting together to complain about composers.

Supertonic: Schweppes (Diatonic: Low-calorie Schweppes.)

Subdominant: Chief officer aboard a submarine.

Subito Piano: Indicates an opportunity for some obscure orchestra player to become a soloist.

Suspension: The state one may find his contract in if he opposes the Major Triad (see above for definition).

Syncopation: A condition incurred from lack of roughage in one's diet.

Tempo: 1. This is where a headache begins. 2. Good choice for a used car.

Tenor: Two hours before a nooner.

Time Signature: What you need from your boss if you forget to clock in.

Tone Cluster: A chordal orgy first discovered by a well-endowed woman pianist leaning forward for a page turn.

Tonic: Medicinal liquid to be consumed before, during, or after a performance. (Diatonic: This is what happens to some musicians.)

Transsectional: An alto who moves to the soprano section.

Transposition: The act of moving the relative pitch of a piece of music that is too low for the basses to a point where it is too high for the sopranos.

Transpositions: 1. Men who wear dresses. 2. An advanced recorder technique where you change from alto to soprano fingering (or vice-versa) in the middle of a piece.

Treble: Women ain't nothin' but.

Trill: The musical equivalent of an epileptic seizure.

Triple Meter: Only rich people should park by these.

Triplet: One of three children, born to one mother very closely in time. If a composer uses a lot of triplets he has probably been taking a fertility drug.

Trotto: an early Italian form of Montezuma's Revenge.

Tuba: A compound word: "Hey, woman! Fetch me another tuba Bryll Cream!"

Twelve-tone Scale: The thing the State Police weigh your tractor-trailer truck with.

Union Rep: A guy who thinks big bands are coming back.

Verse: The part of a tune that's disposable, except to its composer.

Vibrato: Used by singers to hide the fact that they are on the wrong pitch.

Viola D'Amore: A baroque string instrument and coincidentally the hooker Bach lost his virginity to.

Virtuoso: A musician with very high morals. (I know one)

Whole Note: What's due after failing to pay the mortgage for a year.

Wurlitzer: The Ford Pinto of pianos.

Yanni: A man blessed with great hair for music.

24/7: The time signature of the national anthem of India.

In Other Words...

pianissimo

piano

mezzo piano

mezzo forte

FORTE

FORTISSIMO

cresCENDO

DIMINuendo

SForzando

rita r d a n d   o

a c c e l e r ando

stac · ca · to

leeegaaatooo

dolce

fermataaaaaaaaa

PHOTO ALBUM...

THEN. Al Schmitt is one of the most celebrated recording engineers in the history of the music industry. We're with Steve Lukather, lead guitarist, vocalist and songwriter for Toto, a group whose immense international popularity continues to this day, some thirty plus years after their debut.
Left to Right: Me, Al Schmitt, Steve Lukather. June 3, 1991

NOW. We're telling it like it is! With Al Schmitt. 2018

NOW. We're telling it like it is! With Steve Lukather 2019

I was fortunate to join Hugh Laurie in New Orleans to Co-Produce his "Great Performances" special for PBS. A true student of the music of New Orleans, Hugh had the insight and the chops to do honor to the music. March 21, 2011.

Adding NOLA royalty to the effort were the stunning arranger, composer and musician, Allen Toussaint, and the NOLA vocal queen, Irma Thomas. A wonderful moment for me. March 21, 2011.

Goofing with Penelope Spheeris, the director of Wayne's World and the trilogy titled, The Decline of Western Civilization I,II, III. She has a fantastic perspective on the music of today and is whiplash intelligent. A pleasure to spend some time with her. November 22, 2019.

With the fabulous guitarist, Ray Parker, Jr. who's song, "Ghostbusters" from the film, finally answers the question, "Who you gonna call?" November 22, 2019.

In 2013, I had the pleasure of producing Landau Eugene Murphy Jr. Landau was the winner of season six of America's Got Talent, and we created an amazing product filled with new arrangements from the American Songbook to Motown. November 20, 2013. Photo by Barry "Baz" Holmes.

I prefer to record live to two tracks, with no mixing, editing, auto tuning or overdubbing. It's risky business and only a few musicians are good enough to challenge this recording technique. One of those amazing artists is Laith Al Saadi, a terrific songwriter, vocalist and an even more amazing guitarist. Shortly after my production of his album, "Real," Laith was invited to appear on The Voice and ended up fourth. An amazing run. In this photo from our session, Laith (L) is with Lee Sklar (R), one of the most sought after bass players in popular music. Those who know Lee know what his official greeting to everyone is. Believe me, if you haven't given Lee the finger, then you haven't arrived on the scene. I jumped in the back so there would be a bit of variety between the beards. May 28, 2013. Photo by Barry "Baz" Holmes.

While I have had long relationships with most of the artists I produced, my longest relationships were with Barbara Weathers and David Benoit. Barbara is the former lead vocalist with the multi-platinum group, Atlantic Starr. Barbara is a spectacular vocalist and she sang most of the group's greatest hits during her tenure with the band. I have been producing her recordings and her shows for over twenty years. Pianist, composer and arranger David Benoit was at the forefront of jazz fusion and had terrific success with his compositions for close to thirty years. I had the good fortune of producing a great many of his significant hits, most of them recorded live to two tracks. David is one of a very few artists who would ever attempt this recording technique. Left to Right: Me, Barbara Weathers and David Benoit.

On David's projects, I was fortunate to book the best musicians on the planet. Around 2006, for this project, the band contains some of the most sought after musicians in the world. L to R (Standing): Nathan East- Bass, Tim Weisberg - Flutes, Clark Germain- Engineer, Jeffrey Weber- Producer, David Benoit-Piano (Artist),Brian Bromberg - Bass, John "JR" Robinson - Drums, Luis Conte - Percussion, Rick Braun - Trumpet, Andy Suzuki- Sax, Michael Clark - Score Supervisor. L to R (Kneeling): Paul Jackson Jr. - Guitars, Oscar Castro Neves - Acoustic Guitar, Alex Acuna - Percussion.

Barbara Weathers joins me at the Los Angeles Soul Music Festival, a three day R&B music extravaganza that I produced in Los Angeles. Barbara and I are with one of the headliners, the amazing Lalah Hathaway. Left to Right: Me, Lalah Hathaway, Barbara Weathers. July 22, 2016.

In 1984, I produced a large ensemble recording, live to two tracks with Toni Tennille. Most known for her work with The Captain and Tennille, Toni has a staggering voice that literally melted into the classic songs we recorded live to two tracks. We recorded 22 songs in 11 hours, live to two tracks. Toni shined on every one of them. She is a true artist, in every sense of the word. January 19, 1984.

For Toni's recording, I wanted new arrangements made specifically for this project. I leaned very heavily on my good friend Sammy Nestico to handle the arrangements for this project, and boy, did he deliver the goods. Sammy is one of music history's most cherished arrangers. If he's good enough for Count Basie, then he's good enough for me! A true humble genius. Flanking Toni as we listen to a playback in the studio are me (L) and Sammy Nestico (R). Seated is Jerry Weber, my brother, who has worked on a number of my projects, most recently as a fantastic photographer.

Now, this is a killer rhythm section! For composer, pianist, Clifford Lamb's live two track jazz recordings, I assembled these legends, Cindy Blackman Santana (drums) and Buster Williams (Bass) to provide our musical foundation. It worked so well for Clifford, we recorded three projects with them. November 10, 2015.

Here's the full cast and crew for Clifford Lamb's last three albums, beginning in 2015: (L to R) are: Clark Germain (Recording Engineer), Michael Clark (Assoc. Prod./Score Sup.), Jeffrey Weber (Producer), Clifford Lamb (Piano), Cindy Blackman Santana (Drums), Buster Williams (Bass) and Nicholas Payton (Trumpet). November 10, 2015.

With Jon Bon Jovi. June 3, 2013.

With Lionel Ritchie. October 1985.

With the legendary jazz pianist McCoy Tyner, who's album with Jackie McLean I later produced for Blue Note Records. April 7, 1985.

With the wonderful Linda Ronstadt. 1983

*With composer, pianist Lalo Schifrin, best known for creating the Mission
Impossible theme. Here, we're listening to a playback of one of the songs from
the album I am producing and Lalo protects his hands after each take by
donning thick gloves to keep his hands warm. He's simply amazing.
March 30, 1982.*

I love this photo of (L to R): Me, Clark Germain (my recording engineer of 35 years), and Tariqh Akoni, an amazing and extremely popular guitarist who has graced many of my projects. July 17, 2018.

In 1996 I co-produced (along with Michael Lloyd) a wild project for Pat Boone called In A Metal Mood - No More Mr. Nice Guy. We had a large band including horns, background vocals and an extensive rhythm section. Everything was recorded live to two tracks except Pat. I remember that Pat hired the Hell's Angels to ride with him up Sunset Blvd. to Tower Records where he signed the new release in the parking lot, guarded by members of the Angels. And Pat was very definitely Mr. Nice Guy. A pleasure to work with. Left to right: Pat Boone flexing (!), Me, Michael Clark and seated is Clark Germain. October 1996.

In 1981 I produced another live, two track recording with legendary trumpet player, Freddie Hubbard. We filmed the project and it was shown all over the world, way before there was such a thing as YouTube. Great players with music arranged by Allyn Ferguson. July 14, 1981.

With Bill Evans, arguably one of the greatest jazz pianists ever. And that was when my hair was black and didn't come off at night...! August 28, 1977.

I've been involved with some wild bands, including the very first band I was in. Yes, that's me on the drums. We were performing at an end-of-the-school-year party for our UCLA college newspaper, The Daily Bruin. Left to right: Jonathan Kellerman, Me, Martin Rips, and Harold Bronson. Out of the frame: Jim Bickhart and Joseph Hymson (aka Staretski). Bronson went on to co-found the immensely beloved, Rhino Records with Richard Foos and ran it for twenty-four years. Kellerman became a huge New York Times bestselling novelist. Rips and Staretski became writers/producers of quite a few popular network TV shows. May 30, 1970.

Fast forward to 2018, I am with the Ariana Grande band. These guys traveled the world with Grande for four years, and I finally was able to have them on a bunch of my recordings. They are stunning musicians, and the best cats you would ever want to hang with. They make me look like a genius. Left to Right: Andre Frappier (Guitars), Me, Troy Laureta (Arranger, Keyboards), Timothy Bailey (Bass), Joe Otis (Drums).

How's this for a super band! In 1982 I won the lottery when I produced this live recording for legendary music executive Bruce Lundvall. It featured, left to right: Joe Henderson (Tenor Saxophone), Me, Chick Corea (Piano), Nancy Wilson (Vocals), Stanley Clarke (Bass) and Lenny White (Drums). Wow! April 7, 1982.

One of the most heartfelt male vocalists in pop music was Kenny Rankin. No one sounded quite like him then, and no one comes close to him today. I produced an amazing recording with Kenny that featured some of the finest musicians ever! Standing left to right: Robben Ford (Electric Guitars), Vinnie Colaiuta (Drums), Me, Chris Trujillo (Percussion), Kenny Rankin (Vocals), Amy Rankin, Oscar Castro-Neves (Acoustic Guitar), Randy Kerber (Piano). Seated left to right: Lee Sklar (Bass), Gerardo Valez (Percussion). March 21, 1988.

contriButors

I would like to acknowledge and express our sincere gratitude to all those below who so gloriously sank to my level and contributed their wit and wisdom to the regressive, twisted and sometimes evil nature of this nonsense. You have now become part of my family—"tilted in all directions!"

Jeff Ames
Morgan Ames
Kenia Ashby
Bob Belden
David Benoit
Bill Bergman
Randy Bishop
Dave Boruff
Ndugu Chancler
Roger Christian
Kevin Clark
Michael Clark
Jared Cohen
Tom Curtis
Robin Davey
David Del Grosso
Bill Detko
Jim DeVault
Tanika Dozier
Burleigh
  Drummond
Mark Eliasof
Mark Estrada
Charles Feldman
Andre Fischer
Jane Fontana
Judy Francis
Philip Greenwood
Carlos Hatem
Stix Hooper

Bradley Hughes
Scott Jackson
Michael Jochum
Ellen Johnson
Chelsea Jones
Carol Kaye
Robbyn Kirmsee
Tom LeCompte
Michael Madeley
Jack Maher
Alan Marker
Dave Marotta
Don McLeod
John McDaniel
Michael McIntosh
Michael Melvoin
Bill Meyers
Ron Moss
Phil Nemy
Harold Payne
Guy Perchard
Jennifer Phelps
Roger Pigossi
Walfredo Reyes, Jr
Lauren Riedel
Maggie Rieth
Carl Rosenberg
Jay B. Ross
Dave Rouze
Ann Ruckert

James Saez
Doug Scott
Leeland Sklar
Randy Singer
Al Taylor
Robert Tengler
Jon Thomas
Erik Toops
Bill Traut
Chris Trujillo
Marty Walsh
Jon Waxman
Barbara Weathers
Jayme Weber
Jerold Weber
Jordan Weber
Don Winslow
David Witham
Ryan Yezak